SMART FIRMS
IN
SMALL TOWNS

Stuart Rosenfeld
with Philip Shapira and J. Trent Williams

The Aspen Institute
State Policy Program

ISBN: 0-89843-122-0

Table of Contents

Executive Summary

Small and medium-sized enterprises (SMEs) are playing an ever-expanding role in the nation's industrial competitiveness and in localities' economic competitiveness. For most of this century, the prevailing management theory has been that large companies, by supporting economies of scale and specialized resources, were more efficient and more competitive than SMEs. But since the late 1980s, the benefits of large scale have been questioned, in large part because of trends in both customer demand and technological advances being adopted by competitor nations. Mass markets are being replaced by segmented markets, domestic competition by international competition, and standardized products by customized products. New, lower cost, and flexible technologies are more readily available to smaller firms. At the same time, external economies of scale created by new relationships between buyers and suppliers and among firms are supplanting internal economies of scale created by expansion and acquisitions. These economic patterns add to the advantages that smaller firms already have over large firms, such as greater flexibility and ability to innovate and less rigid bureaucracy and hierarchy.

These economic patterns add to the advantages that smaller firms already have over large firms

The new economic environment in which manufacturers are operating suggests a different approach to regional development. Lowest costs are still factors but no longer sufficient for comparative advantage. Quality, delivery, reliability and design have been elevated in importance and now represent the keys to competitiveness. To excel along these dimensions requires that firms continually innovate and "modernize"—use state-of-the-art management practices and process technologies. Modernization refers to the ways that manufacturing firms process material, organize people, use information, integrate systems, and accommodate innovation.

Modernization refers to the ways that manufacturing firms process material, organize people, use information, integrate systems, and accommodate innovation

The new path to development is perhaps best represented by Harvard economist Michael Porter, who asserts that the only way for a region to be competitive is to make sure its industries are competitive. This turns the focus of economic development policy analysis from the individual firm and site to the less conventional units of regional relationships and industry sectors. In this new vision, the traditional three most critical factors—location, location and location—become **innovation, diffusion, and deployment**. It presents rural communities with both a new challenge and new opportunity.

Why are America's small, rural manufacturers so slow to invest in new technologies and adopt best practices?

Yet the research shows that America's small, rural manufacturers are slow to invest in new technologies and adopt best practices. One obstacle to modernization in small establishments is that the **scale of their operations** cannot support specialists and support staff to share the administrative work load and free time for management to think about and act on strategic goals. The typical SME owner or manager works in production, designs the products, and manages and administers the operation. **Labor force skills** also constitute a barrier to modernization. Training programs do not serve small and independent manufacturers well because the manufacturers cannot generate large enough enrollments to justify public expenditures in tailored programs; they do not invest in such training themselves because they underestimate its value to their productivity or fear losing trained workers to competitors. And SMEs have **insufficient intelligence about markets and market trends**. Variations in consumer tastes are both increasing and changing more frequently, and the complexities of entering international markets and dealing with different languages, customs and regulations are confusing to the independent owner. Small firms located in less populated areas are doubly disadvantaged by distance, dispersion and population density. These affect access to information, modernization assistance and support services, capital, and labor markets.

Best Practices, Promising Practices

A few states have had programs or policies aimed at strengthening the comparative advantage of SMEs in place long enough and have a sufficient record of achievement to declare them "best" practices. Although a larger number of even newer programs cannot be labeled best practices yet, they can be considered—based on design and support—"most promising" practices. To be labeled "best state practice," programs must possess certain characteristics, some of which are a function of management and performance and others a function of program design and resources. Some are traits of what is popularly called "Third Wave" economic development: putting the government in the role of wholesaler, avoiding subsidizing market decisions, promoting public-private partnerships, focusing on outcomes rather than process, and adopting market-driven strategies. Under "Third Wave" theory promulgated by the Corporation for Enterprise Development, accountability and feedback are basic elements of all programs.

To enumerate, good programs:

- have scale—the critical mass of resources needed to have a noticeable impact on rural economies;

- are comprehensive—they begin with the firms' needs rather than the expertise of specialists;

- are accessible to firms in communities of all sizes and in all places;

- must be sustainable either because customers value them and are willing to share or pay for the costs of services or the government is willing to make a long-term commitment because the benefits are important to the local economy;

- respond to and stimulate demand;

- complement and expand, not duplicate, private services;

- involve SME owners/managers and labor in their design and planning;

- improve the level of skills and wages and quality of work life in a region; and

- feature a return on investment mentality, an attempt to maximize the value of public sector investments.

State Approaches

States, spurred by original equipment manufacturers' greater emphasis on and higher expectations of their suppliers, finally are beginning to focus on the needs of SMEs, and some have established programs and allocated modest levels of resources aimed at modernization.

State programs and policies to modernize manufacturing in rural areas use seven strategies

State programs and policies to modernize manufacturing in rural areas use seven strategies: brokering, information, assessments, problem-solving, demonstrations, support services, and incentives. Most programs, however, are a hybrid, employing more than one strategy. For example, centers do some outreach, brokers provide information, and support services may be linked to incentives. Thus the examples cited are not intended to compartmentalize a particular program. Each strategy employs some mix of: (1) collective action; (2) one-on-one assistance; (3) general support services; (4) information systems and (5) system and infrastructure to achieve its goals. But most states' modernization efforts are still evolving, trying to find the formulas that work best for their industries, labor forces, and settlement patterns.

A number of new and quite innovative approaches are emerging. For example, as a result of the successes of small manufacturing sectors in Europe and Japan, **interfirm cooperation** has become one of the most widely discussed new concepts in rural industrial development. Rural manufacturers in states as diverse as Oregon, Arkansas, North Carolina and Florida are creating new alliances and tighter business relationships for a variety of purposes: process development, marketing, training and equipment purchase, to name a few.

States have tried various strategies to encourage and stimulate interfirm cooperation

States have tried various strategies to encourage and stimulate interfirm cooperation. One strategy is to create incentives for collaboration, usually as challenge grants for group activities. Another is restructuring existing service programs so that staff become catalysts for network activities. Yet another strategy is supporting individuals or organizations in a community to act as network facilitators and help organize collaborative efforts.

A second emerging approach to modernization is to **organize services** for a specific industrial sector. States are beginning to realize that this approach is the only way they can provide the needed expertise. Some states are considering concentrating their expertise and efforts similar to how the U.S. Departments of Commerce and Agriculture have offices or desks that follow a specific industrial sector or type of product.

A third approach is to **develop industrial extension services**. In 1980, only three colleges had any significant industrial extension service: North Carolina State University, Georgia Tech and Penn State University. During the mid- to late 1980s, industrial extension programs—sometimes called technology extension to provide a more contemporary and modern look—were established in about a dozen states.

A fourth emerging approach is to **link SMEs with technical, community and regional colleges**—the most common sources of non-agricultural technology and technical assistance in rural areas. Regional and technical colleges are continually assuming greater responsibility for economic development and an increasing number are hosts to economic development centers.

The last approach is **youth apprenticeship,** and it is one of the most intriguing new ideas for supporting modernization. Actually, it is new only to the U.S. economy, which has retrofit a program used successfully for generations in Germany and the Scandinavian countries. The idea of an apprenticeship that begins at age 16 and possibly extends through postsecondary education has begun to capture the attention and imagination of U.S. policy-makers.

Steps to Modernization

As evidence of program effectiveness accumulates, both a set of principles for designing state programs and information concerning elements that lead to success are emerging. Many reinforce previously cited characteristics of best practices. The steps are: (1) build constituency and leadership; (2) understand local economies, including linkages among firms, and target sectors; (3) identify and coordinate resources and services; (4) involve SMEs; (5) build scale; and (6) establish procedures for accountability. It is important, for example, to know the state's political environment and build constituencies among government, community organizations, trade associations, labor organizations, SMEs, and large producers. Building an inventory of the state's capabilities and making sure that existing resource providers are involved and coordinated are important parts of the process. And to have the maximum impact, the state ought to be able to map its economy, including the linkages among firms, then target its investments to key critical sectors. It is absolutely essential to involve SMEs early and in all stages, in focus groups and as members of advisory boards, and to allow the customers to guide the process. To achieve scale, modernization must be debated and discussed as an economic development policy, not a technology policy. Finally, accountability procedures must begin to be designed, benchmarks designated from the start and baseline information collected to use later to assess outcomes.

Building an inventory of the state's capabilities and making sure that existing resource providers are involved and coordinated are important parts of the process

In summary, in the best and most promising practices, government agencies **listen** to their clients; **are catalysts** of change and innovation and responsible for a support infrastructure; work to **change attitudes** of SMEs toward each other and the public sector to enhance cooperation, learning and partnerships; and **insure that services are accessible** to firms in small and rural communities. This does, in fact, constitute an ad hoc industrial policy toward which states are leading the federal government and for which bipartisan support is mounting. The best and most promising programs and the experiences of the states establish a frame of reference for formulating new and even more effective national and regional industrial competitiveness strategies.

Chapter 1. Small Manufacturers and Regional Economies: A Policy Guide for Rural Industrial Modernization

Recruitment of branch plants has been the bread and butter of rural growth, particularly in southern and mid-Atlantic states, for decades. But the world is changing. The stakes (and costs) of "winning" the industrial recruitment sweepstakes are rising dramatically as states are forced to offer more incentives to compete for a diminishing number of new plants. Competition for plants is becoming more intense than ever before, and firms are shifting from lower costs to product differentiation for their competitive advantage. Firms that seek lower labor costs still can go to lesser developed regions; those seeking close proximity to suppliers and skilled labor will gravitate toward urban locations. Thus, many rural sites are losing their historic cost advantages.

Yet industrial recruitment continues unabated in many parts of the nation. Even North Carolina, one of the most successful recruiters, is hit hard by plant relocations and shutdowns. In February 1992, for example, a Procter Silex plant in Southern Pines, North Carolina, announced it was moving its production to Mexico, where labor costs are $35 per week. In 1970, the United States was home to 20 percent of the machine tool industry, much of which was small, family-owned, and rural. But the U.S. share is only 6 percent today (ranking sixth among nations), and half of those firms in the U.S. are foreign-owned.

The economic development profession was mildly shaken in the late 1970s, when David Birch's research revealed the large share of new jobs created by small businesses. States responded with a plethora of new programs, most quite small in scale, to support new business formation. Programs to assist entrepreneurs with ideas that could grow into major industries through venture capital and incubation of infant firms proliferated. And new programs to assist with industry expansions were created to reward plants for major increases in employment.

Recruitment and new business formation leave an increasingly conspicuous gap in economic development policy

These two approaches to industrial development—recruitment and new business formation—leave an increasingly conspicuous gap in economic development policy, which is the large number of manufacturers located in rural areas. The vast majority of manufacturers are neither branches of large corporations nor new firms. About 90 percent are small or medium-sized (fewer than 250 employees), independently owned enterprises that produce parts and components for original equipment manufacturers (OEMs) and fill important niche markets for increasingly discriminating customers. These companies are often referred to as **SMEs (small and medium-size enterprises)**. More than 350,000 SMEs in the United States employ about eight million workers, which accounts for about two-fifths of the nation's manufacturing employment. These firms contribute about one-third of the value added in manufacturing. Across the nation, about one-fifth of all SMEs are located in non-metropolitan counties, but that varies considerably by region. In the deep South states of Alabama, Georgia and Mississippi, for example, 51 percent of manufacturing plants are located in non-metropolitan counties where they employ 41 percent, 38 percent and 32 percent, respectively, of their state's non-agricultural workforce. While some of these smaller plants are branches of large corporations, most are independently owned.

Despite the significant contribution of small and medium-sized manufacturing enterprises to regional economies, they have received precious little attention from economic development officials. The Congressional Office of Technology Assessment reported that existing technology extension services for manufacturing (defined as services aimed at transferring technology, modernizing manufacturing processes, and/or improving the productivity and profitability of businesses) reach fewer than 2 percent of the nation's firms each year. Extension or technology services for SMEs are particularly rare in traditional non-durable goods industries such as apparel, food processing and furniture, which predominate in rural areas. In fact, most states are unable to provide a comprehensive accounting—or even a head count—of their very small manufacturers. The few programs that are aimed at SMEs are far too modest and limited in scope to meet SMEs' needs. On the other hand, small firms, generally, are too caught up in day-to-day problems to be able to articulate their needs in ways that translate into services.

The few programs that are aimed at SMEs are far too modest and limited in scope to meet SME's needs

Small supplier firms play an important role in the nation's industrial competitiveness and in local economic growth. If a healthy manufacturing sector is vital to a region's economy—an argument that has been made convincingly by many economic experts in recent years—then the region's supplier firms must be able to meet the demand of its final producers and to compete effectively in national and, increasingly, global markets. Over the past few years, OEMs have been undergoing what the popular press refers to as **"hollowing out,"** the process of contracting more and more production work to subcontractors. At the same time, OEMs have been reducing the number of their subcontractors. The two practices have created twin pressures on SMEs. First, they must meet increasingly demanding OEM requirements. Second, they are pushed to diversify into new areas of business. Lowest cost is still a factor but it is no longer a sufficient advantage. It has been edged out as quality, delivery, reliability and design have been elevated in importance and are now the **keys to competitiveness**.

In a word, the process is "modernization"—those state-of-the-art management practices and process technologies that give producers significant advantages over their competitors in the marketplace. Modernization focuses on the ways that manufacturing firms process material, organize people, use information, integrate systems, and accommodate innovation. As defined by Georgia Tech professor Philip Shapira in a report to the National Institute of Standards and Technology, industrial modernization means "the application of upgraded technologies, design, manufacturing, and marketing methods, improved quality control systems, and enhanced management and training to raise productivity, quality, product performance, workforce skills, and company manufacturing capabilities to best practice international levels."

Today's economic environment makes it imperative that manufacturers modernize and suggests a new approach to regional development. The new path is perhaps best represented by Harvard economist Michael Porter, who asserts that the only way for a region to be competitive is to make sure its industries are competitive. This turns the focus of economic development policy analysis from the individual firm and site to the units of regional relationships and industry sectors. The three traditionally most critical factors—location, location and location—become **innovation, diffusion and deployment** in this new vision. This new theory of economic competitiveness presents rural communities with both a new challenge and new opportunities.

Past Efforts to Modernize Manufacturing

Modernization is hardly a new concept in rural areas. Policies to acquaint farmers with and persuade them to use new technologies date back to the close of the 19th Century. Land grant colleges established agricultural experiment stations to develop new mechanized technologies and farming practices while states, supported by banks and private foundations, sponsored county agents whose job it was to ensure that the latest technologies were widely disseminated and adopted. The federal government expanded and institutionalized modernization programs. In 1914, when the Smith-Lever Act authorizing cooperative extension services through land grant colleges was enacted, industrialization was already moving ahead; in some rural counties, manufacturing was beginning to represent major portions of local economies. Congress recognized this expansion of employment opportunities as good for rural regions. As a result, Section 8 of the Smith-Lever Act authorized the Secretary of Agriculture to provide assistance and counseling that introduced industry as a farm income supplement in communities where the concentration of farm families was low or farming was unproductive.

For the next half century, despite accelerating industrialization, the vast majority of public sector modernization efforts were directed at farming. By 1950, 25 percent of the workforce was employed in manufacturing and less than 12 percent in farming. A few states began to operate industrial outreach programs in the late 1950s. But such efforts were on a very small scale, tightly linked to universities rather than dispersed, and aimed more at industrial recruitment than assisting existing firms. With no social infrastructure to facilitate the interchange of ideas—similar to what was provided to farmers through the Grange, the Farmer's Union and Future Farmers of America—and with no cooperatives to link manufacturers to one another as agricultural cooperatives did for farmers, there were few opportunities for manufacturers to learn from each other. Furthermore, industrial education lacked the pedagogical focus on technological change and experimentation of vocational agriculture: Youth enrolled in vocational agriculture learned the value of innovation, experimentation and cooperation and to make decisions. Youth enrolled in industrial programs merely learned to operate equipment and follow instructions.

A few states began to operate industrial outreach programs in the late 1950s

In 1961, President Kennedy proposed a Civilian Industrial Technology Program targeted at industries that historically underinvested in research and development, but his program failed to get congressional support. As outlined by Secretary of Commerce Luther H. Hodges, the program would have provided "an industry university 'extension service' patterned after the agriculture extension service," for collecting and distributing technical information, and otherwise stimulating industrial research.[1] At that time, much as today, business argued against "industrial policy." With the United States in the driver's seat in world industrial production and most of the rest of the industrialized world still recovering from the ravages of World War II, public policies did indeed seem less urgent. In the 1990s, however, global conditions are quite different. The playing field today is measured, more often than not, in meters, not yards. How has industry and how have the states responded to the new economy and new markets?

The State of Rural Industry

According to comparative data on the utilization of new technologies, U.S. industry lags behind many of its competitor nations. Research on the state of business competitiveness consistently reveals disparities between the proportions of manufacturers that use or intend to use advanced manufacturing techniques and technologies in the United States relating to Japan, Germany, Sweden, or Italy. While these numbers are to some extent a function of industrial compositions, they also are a harbinger of the future competitiveness of rural America.

Defining "advanced technology": Advanced technologies are generally defined by the application of programmable actions and decisions, and they include a range of computer-aided and computer-integrated operations, such as computer numerically controlled machines (CNC); robotics; programmable logic controllers; automated material identification and moving and inspection equipment; and computer-aided design (CAD), engineering (CAE); and manufacturing (CAM). When related automated machines are linked together to produce a part, the entire process is called a flexible manufacturing cell (FMC). When cells are combined to manufacture an end product, the result is called a flexible manufacturing system (FMS). And when the production process is linked by computer to ordering, production control, inventory, sales and administration, the production unit is called computer-integrated manufacturing (CIM).

Advanced technology, in its broadest sense, is more than production processes

Most industry executives and analysts do not limit the term technology to hard technologies as defined by programmable machines. Scientific management methods such as statistical process control (SPC), total quality management (TQM), just-in-time inventory (JIT) and materials requirements planning (MRP) are generally considered advanced technologies as well. But advanced technology, in its broadest sense, is more than production processes. It entails the entire manufacturing operation, which includes not only the production process but new forms of relationships to suppliers and customers, improved training, market intelligence and sensing devices and creative financing. An advanced, or "modern," firm knows its markets, understands the nature of the competitive environment in which it operates and utilizes appropriate technologies and techniques to continually improve and innovate.

Classifying manufacturing: The federal government categorizes manufacturing firms based on their principal products and according to a scheme called the Standard Industry Classification (SIC). Textile mill products, printing and publishing, fabricated metal products and electric and electronic equipment are examples of SICs at the most general, or two-digit, level. Under each two-digit category, three-digit subcategories further classify the product. Electric and electronic equipment, for instance, includes electrical industrial apparatus, household appliances and communications equipment. These are distinguished even further at a four-digit level. Communications equipment includes, for example, telephone and telegraph apparatus, and radio and television communication equipment.

While useful for economic analysis, these classifications are not as helpful in understanding a firm's technology needs. Manufacturing is further distinguished by manufacturing processes and organizational structures rather than just products. Continuous process plants, such as those in the chemical and petroleum industries, are usually quite capital-intensive and located near key natural resources, generally in rural areas. Such plants are not likely to use CNC machines, but they were among the first industries to use computers to control, monitor and test production. Mass producers, such as final assemblers of consumer products, are generally the largest and more integrated vertically and require abundant supplies of less-skilled labor. They tend to be major customers for robotics, to replace repetitive, heavy, and sometimes hazardous manual motions, and for automated materials handling equipment. Limited batch manufacturers produce customized or specialized items in small numbers, such as special cabinets for a building or storage bins for a new plant. Job shops produce highly specialized machine parts, tools or equipment and tend to require the most skilled workers. Many small batch plants and job shops, often operated by entrepreneurs, produce for highly specialized market niches, such as knitwear or biotechnology firms, and their competitiveness depends on a unique product or highly specialized expertise.

Table 1
Rates of Adoption of Technologies in the Rural South by Firm Size, 1989 (%)

Technology	Number of Employees		
	1–49	50–249	250 or More
CAD	23	47	72
CAE	17	38	41
CNC Machines	20	42	17
Robots	3	7	17
Programmable Controllers	22	54	61
Automated Materials Handling	9	25	56
Shop Floor Microcomputers	12	44	72
Automated Data Collection	6	23	61
Automated Inspection	9	13	39
Statistical Process Control	18	45	94
Group Technology	4	14	39
Flexible Manufacturing Cells	4	16	50

Source: Survey conducted by the Consortium for Manufacturing Competitiveness, 1989.

Levels of technology penetration: Many advanced technologies and techniques—proven in practice, available commercially for decades, and considered vital to competitiveness—are seldom found in SMEs. A national survey of manufacturers by the Department of Commerce in 1988, for example, found that whereas 83 percent of large companies (more than 500 employees) use CAD, only 30 percent of small companies (fewer than 50 employees) use CAD; 78 percent of large companies use but only 23 percent of small firms use programmable logic controllers. A similar survey restricted to the rural South (Table 1) found that only 23 percent of firms with fewer than 50 employees but 72 percent of firms with more than 250 employees use CAD, 20 percent of the small firms but 67 percent of the large firms use CNC machines; and 18 percent of the small firms but 94 percent of the large firms use statistical process control.[2]

What are these rates of utilization expected to look like in two to three years? Are more and more firms going to modernize? In both surveys, firms not already using a particular technology were asked whether they were planning to adopt it in subsequent years (two years in the national survey and two to three years in the southern rural survey). The percentages planning automation was even lower. Only 11 percent of non-CAD users were planning to introduce CAD; only eight percent of rural southern firms and five percent of all manufacturers not using any CNC equipment were planning to; and only 18 percent not using statistical process control were intending to in the next few years. A regional survey conducted in the Midwest and state surveys in Virginia and West Virginia corroborate the data. Despite the exhortations of equipment producers, trade associations, industry journals, and experts, American industry has not been quick to embrace new technologies and techniques.

Characterizing regional differences: Historically, the South's rural areas have attracted the most routine production, primarily in labor-intensive, non-durable goods industries. About one-third of the region's manufacturing workforce is employed in textiles or apparel and another nine percent in wood products. Although these are generally perceived as large, vertically integrated industries, there are many SMEs supplying the larger industries or producing for specialty markets. The Northeast's industrial base is the most urbanized of any in the country. But even in this region, thousands of small town job shops and suppliers feed such major industrial hubs as Detroit, Pittsburgh, Cleveland, Erie, Dayton, Philadelphia and Boston. Dispersed suppliers to the automotive or industrial equipment sector, dominated by giants such as Ford, General Motors, General Electric, and Westinghouse, provide thousands of highly skilled jobs. In the Northwest, the wood products industry dominates rural areas.

Thousands of small town job shops and suppliers feed major industrial hubs

Many Midwestern SMEs were founded by second generation farmers transferring mechanical skills from food production to another product.

Such generalizations cannot be taken too far and are only useful for making regional comparisons and looking for opportunities for **sector-specific investments**. Each region is a mosaic, with pockets of strength in nearly every industry found in the region somewhere. There are, for example, major machine tool centers near Birmingham, Alabama, wood products in southern Appalachia, and apparel firms remain strong in some parts of New England and southern California.

Regional patterns among the owners and managers of SMEs also exist. In the South and Midwest, it is quite common for the owner to come from a farm family; in the Northeast, the owner is more likely to be a skilled craftsman or the son (and, in too rare instances, daughter) of a skilled craftsman from a large industrial plant. About 60 percent of small, rural firms are family-owned. Northern firms, because of their ties to large, unionized companies, are also more apt to be union shops and members of a trade association than southern or midwestern SMEs.

Competitiveness of Rural SMEs

For the first three-quarters of the 20th Century, the prevailing management theory was that large companies, through economies of scale and specialized resources, were more efficient and competitive than SMEs. Industrial modernization became associated with urban centers and was believed to be represented most effectively and efficiently by the large-scale, vertically integrated, hierarchical corporation, not the family-owned, skilled, specialized, artisan manufacturer. Small manufacturers were, by conventional definition, not modern or progressive.

But since the late 1980s, the benefits of large-scale operations have been questioned, in large part because of **trends in both customer demand and technological advances** adopted by competitor nations. Segmented markets, international competition, and customized products are replacing mass markets, domestic competition and standardized products. New, lower cost technologies are becoming more readily available to smaller firms. At the same time, external economies of scale created by new relationships between buyers and suppliers and among firms are supplanting internal economies of scale created through expansions and acquisitions.

These economic patterns add to advantages such as greater flexibility and ability to innovate and less rigid bureaucracies and hierarchy that smaller firms have over large firms. A new report prepared for the Department of Defense by Lehigh University contends that **agile manufacturing**—the term coined for this emerging form of production—"favors smaller scale, modular production facilities, and cooperation between enterprises." Even the largest corporations are using decentralization and outsourcing in order to exploit the advantages of smaller scale. Another advantage of SMEs, especially when they are family- or locally owned, is that they tend to have strong ties to their communities and to be more stable contributors to the local economy. They are far less likely to change production sites to lower their costs. All of this means greater opportunities for SMEs and for their host towns and small cities.

SMEs tend to have strong ties to their communities and to be more stable contributors to the local economy

Deterrents to Rural Industrial Modernization

With all of these new opportunities, why are America's small, rural manufacturers so slow to invest in new technologies and adopt best practices? The most common reason cited in the 1989 rural South surveys was that management did not believe the returns would justify the investments. The second most common reason differed for small and medium-sized firms; the smallest firms (under 50 employees) cited access to capital, while the medium-sized firms (50–249 employees) named lack of appropriate technology. "Small" and "rural" pose different, albeit overlapping, sets of obstacles. Problems that are endemic to small scale and independently owned firms are exacerbated by diseconomies of scale and distance from resources in less populated areas.

The consequences of small size and independence: One obstacle to modernization in small establishments is that the scale of their operations cannot support administrative specialists whose work gives management time to develop and carry out strategic goals. Typically, SME owners or managers work in production, design products, and manage and administer operations. Because they have so many responsibilities, most SME owners or managers lack the time or expertise to do what is necessary to remain competitive: monitor technological and market **developments and trends**, develop **strategic plans**, carry out **product or process development**, and analyze new **investment opportunities** carefully. A national survey conducted by the John F. Kennedy School of Government at Harvard found that 40 percent of firms not using computer-assisted equipment blamed lack of information for their non-use, while almost 70 percent cited the inability to assess outcomes as the reason. The vast majority of small firm owners and managers are far too busy solving day-to-day production problems and trying to maintain a positive cash flow to spend time thinking about long-term planning or scanning national economic trends, much less staying abreast of the latest technologies.

Most SME owners or managers lack the time or expertise to do what is necessary to remain competitive

The **fiercely independent nature** of many SME owners poses a second obstacle to modernization. As modern day versions of the Jeffersonian yeoman farmer, owners are wary of universities that preach from their "ivory towers," government agencies that force them to comply with regulations and fill out too many forms, and banks that are neither understanding nor sympathetic to their needs. A large number of SMEs do not even return industrial directory forms and consequently are omitted from listings in state publications. They do not join chambers of commerce, local business groups, or trade associations, and they have little time for management seminars.

Labor force skills constitute a third barrier to modernization, although, according to surveys, this not as formidable a barrier as education reformers claim. Only 21 percent of SMEs ranked the lack of a skilled workforce high among barriers to modernization. Although many critics blame the decline of U.S. industry on poor workforce skills, studies by the National Commission on Education and the Economy and by the Economic Policy Center argue that American businesses are not organized to use higher skills and implicitly prefer low wages to high skills. Furthermore, SMEs generally do not pay high enough wages or provide good enough benefits to attract highly skilled workers or, when they do acquire or train skilled workers, to prevent high turnover.

Nevertheless, small and independent manufacturers are not well served by training programs because the programs do not generate enrollments large enough to justify public expenditures in tailored programs. For example, fourteen small precision metal fabricators in the Piedmont region of North Carolina were unable to find training programs in the use of new computer-controlled brake presses for their operators. Only by joining together and representing themselves as a large firm would any community college take them seriously. Also, the manufacturers do not invest in such training themselves because they underestimate its value to their productivity or fear losing trained workers to competitors.

Succession poses a fourth problem. According to a national survey, less than 30 percent of family businesses succeed to a second generation. In closely held businesses with no apparent heir and no succession plans—even when capital is available—older CEOs are reluctant to make long-term investments in their companies. With no compelling reason to modernize, an aging owner is likely to take the profits out and invest them elsewhere. This is a particularly troublesome problem in the machine tool industry, which is predominantly family-owned. Most experts believe that succession ought to be planned at least ten years before retirement, yet few SMEs make such plans, either due to ignorance of the potential problem or to avoid what can be difficult and emotional family issues.

Few SMEs make such plans, either due to ignorance of the potential problem or to avoid what can be difficult and emotional family issues

Finally, SMEs **lack sufficient intelligence** about markets and market trends. Variations in consumer tastes are both increasing and changing more rapidly than they did years ago. For example, a decade ago, generic brands filled supermarket shelves; today, consumers can choose from among low salt, low fat, low cholesterol, and low calorie for a given product. Seasons in the apparel industry have increased from four to eight per year. Furthermore, the complexities of entering international markets and dealing with different languages, customs and regulations can be confusing to the independent owner. Market information is available, but it is often too costly or too time-consuming for small manufacturers to access; most states try to provide technical and financial assistance, but get few takers. Barriers to exporting, according to an extensive study by Bill Nothdurft, tend to be internal to the firms. Owners and managers lack either the time or inclination to export. Part of the problem is that marketing is perceived as a separate and distinctive program, not as an integral part of industrial modernization. Instead of using markets to drive technology adoption and technologies to provide opportunities to enter new markets, the two are divorced from one another at company policy and program levels.

Ruralness: Small firms located in less populated areas are doubly disadvantaged by geographic conditions— distance, dispersion, and population density. These conditions affect access to and delivery of information as well as access to and demand for modernization assistance and support services.

Good **information** is difficult to use unless there is someone to help access, translate and evaluate it. Few small firms will avail themselves of information systems, no matter how good they are. Under these conditions, vendors who knock on doors are the most common source of information about new technologies. Lacking objective information about investment alternatives or knowledge of how to integrate a vendor's equipment into the firm's overall production system and its long-term strategy, the firm is likely to invest piecemeal rather than systematically toward an integrated system.

The **social environment** in very remote areas is not conducive to owners sharing information among themselves. Despite the popular image of close-knit small towns with church picnics and bazaars, small town manufacturers, in fact, have limited social or professional interaction with peers and few opportunities to learn from their competitors, customers or suppliers. They rarely get together to talk about production matters, such as common problems or opportunities. One reason for this lack of communication is that they view nearby firms as potential competitors for the same markets. Even when willing to talk to their perceived competitors, lengthy travel times and absence of institutional settings for regular interactions are inhibiting such exchanges.

In Europe, industry associations provide a social environment and useful information. But in the United States, the main mission of industry associations is lobbying, not providing services or technical information, and rural chapters are scarce. This is not to say that small town associations do not work. Successes of local rural industry associations suggest that many owners or managers of firms, though still wary of competition, want the opportunity to exchange information and socialize. In rural northwestern Minnesota and eastern North and South Dakota, dozens of owners and managers drive an hour or more to attend monthly meetings of the Tri-State Manufacturers Association, formed in 1989. Firms in the metals industries in southern Arkansas, working together as the Metalworking Connection, are doing the same.

This is not to say that small town associations do not work

Distance from resources such as staff, students and technologies located at colleges and universities, large labor pools, financial institutions, and transportation hubs also hamper rural SME modernization efforts. Most firms on Michigan's northern peninsula, for example, are located at least eight hours by ground transportation from a major city, and there are few technical resources able to reach those firms easily. Trade shows and professional conferences—events that urban manufacturers take for granted—are rarely attended by isolated firms. Just a few industrial extension services provide substantial rural outreach. Only about 10 percent of the rural South SMEs surveyed reported that they received help with technological issues from colleges, universities or state agencies.

About 10 percent of the rural South SMEs surveyed reported that they received help with technological issues

Nearly two-thirds had never received assistance from any public sector institution or agency. Finally, the **market system** itself works to the disadvantage of rural firms even when services are available. With fewer possibilities from which to choose for services, there is less competition to drive up quality and less chance that the service will fit a firm's special needs.

Rural SME owners also lack sufficient and timely **access to capital**. Thirty-seven percent of firms in the rural South cited lack of capital as a reason for not investing in new technology. In a survey of firms in rural Virginia, more than 40 percent cited capital as an obstacle, and at a meeting of small and rural manufacturers in Oklahoma in the fall of 1991, participants cited financing as their most pressing problem. Too many bankers in rural areas are unfamiliar with the value of production technologies or technology-based accounting practices and are reluctant to consider strategic benefits, and remote SMEs have few alternatives. Capital gaps for modernizing SMEs are more likely to exist in the area of working capital than investment in plant or equipment. Equipment vendors anxious to make sales will generally provide their own financing. But this leaves the small firm with a number of small loans secured by its new assets, no funds for working capital to pay operating costs and receivables until the investments begin to pay off, and few local banks willing to make those loans. The owner of an established and highly successful plant in rural Arkansas, trying to begin another business in rural North Carolina, told the 1991 annual meeting of the Southern Growth Policies Board that even his orders in hand did not convince banks to provide short-term working capital.

Labor markets are much more restricted in rural areas. Engineering and business college graduates are drawn to cities where, if internal opportunities for advancement are not available, there are other opportunities. Moreover, concerns of working spouses exacerbate the problems of rural plants in recruiting quality workers. Even when an excellent opportunity is available and the recruit is willing to relocate in rural America, the offer may be rejected because there may not be suitable or acceptable employment for a professional spouse. Thus, rural manufacturers generally have a great deal of difficulty attracting professional or technical staff, unless the location is within reasonable commuting distance of large labor markets or there are compelling personal reasons, such as local family ties or health considerations. When MidSouth Electric decided to build a new plant in Anneville, Kentucky, and needed to recruit engineers, it found that, for the most part, its labor market was limited to Kentuckians. And most recruits chose to live in London, a larger city with better schools and more amenities that is about 30 miles away. For a rapidly growing company in Red Lake, Minnesota, recruitment is even more problematic. The company's owner sees little hope of attracting an engineer to a town of 200 that is located 40 miles from a "city" of 9,000.

Last, **perceptions** about rural America affect technology-based development. First, there is still a widely held perception that rural regions can remain agricultural or farm communities. Therefore, local capital is invested in agricultural projects rather than industrial development. SMEs get little help from local or multi-county development agencies or community organizations, which are dominated by agricultural interests or proponents of industrial recruitment. Another perception, this one advanced by economists and developers in urban areas, is that growth theories are based on industrial agglomeration. They contend that competitiveness depends on large numbers of firms located near one another, and that economies of scale dictate that public services concentrate on industrial agglomerations. This would direct resources to concentrations, which, of course, are rare in rural areas.

Local capital is invested in agricultural projects rather than industrial development

All the barriers and obstacles to modernization notwithstanding, some small, rural manufacturers can boast of being among the best in the world. They can produce high quality, well-designed goods and meet demanding delivery schedules. But will there be enough of these manufacturers that can match the benchmarks set by the world's exemplary firms to generate self-sustaining rural development? What can state and local governments do to help their small and medium-sized manufacturers compete with the best in their respective industries?

The Need for Rural Industrial Modernization Programs

U.S. industry and SMEs have operated for years with little support, and the public sector has shown little concern for modernization. Investments in new technologies have been assumed to be internal, market-driven, management decisions that the federal government has tried to influence only at the margins, such as through investment tax credits and procurement policies. Competitiveness in civilian industry has not been considered sufficient cause for government intervention. Until the 1980s, competitiveness meant location and was a domestic concern of states and localities. Plants received attention when considering a new location or expansion. But SMEs, which individually have not interested governments because they do not generate large numbers of new jobs in one fell swoop, have been neglected. Yet, as stated earlier, small and medium-sized establishments collectively generate one-third of the value added in the nation's manufacturing and employ nearly two-fifths of the industrial workforce.

State governments have paid scant heed to SME's needs

Both the providers and consumers of technology and innovation must share blame for the paucity of technology services. On the one hand, SMEs have not demanded enough in the way of services. Perhaps it is because they are unaware of the problems they are, or soon will be, facing or the potential value of new technologies. Or perhaps it is because SMEs have been neglected for so long they view government as an adversary, creating barriers through rules and regulations that come with time-consuming requests for information and are designed for large corporations. State governments have paid scant heed to SMEs' needs, focusing instead on branch plants which are able to demand and get subsidies in the form of training, reduced taxes, free or low-cost sites or on new small businesses which get subsidized loans, incubator space or technical advice. Universities have not attended to SMEs' needs, either, looking instead to the more lucrative contracts and more technologically demanding needs of large corporations. And suppliers of technology services charge SMEs premium prices because their orders are small.

Chapter 2. "Best" Practices, "Promising" Practices

Growing interest in the manufacturing competence of the SME as an instrument of economic development has led states to adopt a plethora of new initiatives. Most of the **programs can be categorized along four dimensions**: their organization or institutional base; their medium for interacting with firms; how they are accessed; and their approach (see Figure 1). These state programs are differentiated according to: (1) whether they are organized by or located in a university, college, state agency or department, or as an independent; (2) their reliance on individuals/experts, institutions/centers, or information/telecommunications; (3) whether they offer on-site visits with clients or expect clients to come to a central location; and (4) if they work with firms one-on-one or collectively.

A few states have pioneered programs or policies aimed at strengthening the comparative advantage of SMEs long enough and with a sufficient record of achievement to declare them **"best" practices**. A growing

Figure 1
Typology of New State Programs

Organization	• Independent • University or college • State agency or department
Medium	• Individuals/experts • Institutions/centers • Information/telecommunications
Access	• Magnet/"come to" • Mobile/"go to"
Approach	• Individual firm/one-on-one • Groups of firms/collective

number of newer programs, which cannot yet be labeled best practices, can be considered—based on their design and support—**"most promising" practices**. Eight programs can be considered as representative of some aspect of best practice: Minnesota Technology, Inc.; the Northern Economic Initiatives Center; Pennsylvania's Industrial Resource Centers; Kentucky's Community Colleges and the Center for Robotics and Manufacturing Systems; Georgia Tech's Economic Development Laboratory; Texas' Technology Business Development Center; the Consortium for Manufacturing Competitiveness; Maine's Center for Technology Transfer; Oregon's industrial networks; Kansas' Mid-America Manufacturing Technology Center; Arkansas' Science & Technology Authority; and Indiana's Regional Technology Councils.

Minnesota Technology, Inc., one of the newer programs, is decentralized and accessible to firms in remote areas, complements existing services, focuses on strategic goals rather than specific problems, holds its programs accountable and requires feedback, and has scale—at least by U.S. standards. The **Northern Economic Initiatives Center**, based in Michigan's upper peninsula, is not a state-wide program but a rural, regional, state-supported program. It has a sectoral focus, builds alliances with other organizations, and is comprehensive.[3] **Pennsylvania's Industrial Resource Centers** are regionally based, clearly market-driven, well-monitored, evaluated, and well-funded. **Kentucky** has developed a relationship between the university and the state's **community colleges and its mobile units.** **Georgia Tech's Economic Development Laboratory** has one of the nation's most mature programs, with a well-established network of engineers in 11 field offices who work with industries, assess their needs, and solve problems; it has sustainability, a clear mission, outreach and support. **Texas' Engineering Experiment Station's Technology Development Business Center** includes modernization as part of overall economic development. The **Consortium for Manufacturing Competitiveness** demonstrates the effectiveness of two-year colleges in assisting SMEs to modernize. While traditionally the colleges have approached modernization strictly through training, many possess the technical expertise, outreach, accessibility in rural areas, and credibility among manufacturers to become centers for technology extension and demonstration. This 14-state project is included as a best practice because a few of its member states have developed policies that use two-year colleges as manufacturing technology centers. **Maine's Center for Technology Transfer** is an example of state industrial policy focused on SMEs in two important industries, metals and electronics.

Other programs, too new to be judged "best practices," possess the design, process and support to suggest that they may, in short time, become best practices. **Oregon** has taken the most systematic and innovative approach to modernization, focusing on its important forestry industries and giving the private sector a major role. The **Mid-America Manufacturing Technology Center** in Kansas is one of the newest federally funded centers and is trying to address the needs of firms in remote areas. **Arkansas** is a relatively poor state that must build on what it has and find ways to coordinate existing resources, but it is also a state willing to try new ideas. **Indiana's Business Modernization and Technology Corporation** uses the regional centers as liaisons and introduces networks to bring together firms and service providers.

These four promising new practices, which are described in case studies, were chosen to demonstrate the diversity of approaches that can be taken. But there are other notable state programs with promise and which could just as readily have been selected. For example, **Maryland's Department of Economic and Employment Development** has established Regional Technology Councils, provided $100,000 each for directors and support, and charged the councils with coordinating efforts around technology development and modernization. Council directors have been trained in manufacturing network development and are working toward establishing an environment that supports collaboration. **Tennessee's Department of Economic and Community Development**, with a technology extension grant from the National Institute of Standards and Technology (NIST), has designed a pilot system that

There are other notable state programs with promise and which could just as readily have been selected

builds on NIST's primary mission—using the resources of the federal labs to help solve industrial problems. The state has contracted with the University of Tennessee's Center for Industrial Services to manage the program. During the first and only year of federal funding, the program assisted 18 businesses and put in place two Cooperative Research and Development Agreements (or "CRADAs," authorized under the federal Stevenson-Wydler Act) with Martin Marietta Energy Systems, Inc. One agreement is to assist Tennessee firms with environmental problems, and the other establishes a Precision Manufacturing Technology Program for the 1,782 manufacturers in the state that utilize machining. **Oklahoma** is in the midst of an exemplary process of planning for an extension service (with an NIST grant) which, based on the widespread support among business and government and educational institutions and state support provided through the Oklahoma Center for the Advancement of Science and Technology (OCAST), may become an outstanding program. The plan calls for a multi-tiered program with the first tier the broker/agents who identify clients and assess their needs, a second tier of technical experts to provide the assistance, and a third tier of industry sector consultants with knowledge of trends and market opportunities.

Defining "Best" or "Most Promising" Practice

On what bases were these examples of best and most promising practices chosen? Most efforts are still relatively new, and states have been unable to agree on appropriate outcomes and measures. Unlike more conventional economic development programs, whose results can be measured in terms of new jobs created, new business start-ups, or loans repaid, modernization benefits to the state are more obscure. Therefore, the qualities of "best practices" are more difficult to define, much less measure, so few sound evaluations exist. Yet these programs must be held accountable, and state and local governments must be able to assess their new programs' results. In the absence of such measurements, program administrators count numbers of interactions with SMEs or collect

Modernization benefits to the state are more obscure

testimonials from client firms and present those as evidence of performance. Even cooperative extension uses simple counts of interactions with clients as its primary measure of success.

We believe, however, that best state programs possess **certain characteristics**, some of which are a function of management and performance and others of program design and resources. Some are characteristics of what has been termed "Third Wave" economic development: putting the government in the role of wholesaler, avoiding subsidizing market decisions, promoting public-private partnerships, focusing on outcomes rather than process, and adopting market-driven strategies. Under "Third Wave" theory fostered by the Corporation for Enterprise Development, accountability and feedback are basic elements of all programs.

Good programs have scale: Scale is the critical mass of resources needed to have a noticeable impact on rural economies. Addressing the needs of a small number of firms, even if the intervention is highly successful, is not likely to change the local employment situation or increase local wealth. Very few, if any, state or federal programs in the United States are of a scale sufficient to make a difference in a region's economy. Furthermore, it is unlikely that any program will achieve competitiveness on a significant scale until modernization is considered part of conventional economic development policy, not a separate technology, or fringe, policy that is subject to budget cuts at the first economic downturn. Only a handful of modernization programs have annual state appropriations of more than $1 million. Pennsylvania's eight Industrial Resource Centers were given $10 million each and the Greater Minnesota Corporation was promised $95 million in start-up funds, but these are rare exceptions. Of the more than 40 technology extension programs surveyed by the National Governors' Association in 1991, half have fewer than 10 professional staff members. In contrast, Denmark, a nation of five million people, has invested $25 million in a new industrial networking program and operates Technology Information Centers in every county; its firms support a 1,300-person technological institute.

Only a handful of modernization programs have annual state appropriations of more than $1 million

With only one or two exceptions, manufacturing network programs in the states have started with less than 1 percent of Denmark's budget.

Good programs are comprehensive: SMEs are confused by the surfeit of public programs knocking on their doors that have only one "product line." Technology programs advise them to change their processes, business assistance programs advise them to change their accounting procedures, technical colleges offer training and continuing education, and export programs counsel them on how to enter overseas markets. What SMEs need is comprehensive strategic planning that begins by considering all of their needs, weighs the alternatives, then sets priorities. The most common practice is for a program to combine technology and training; few are able to be more comprehensive. For example, the Northern Economic Initiatives Center provides **one-stop shopping** by offering marketing, office modernization, industrial design and management assistance to firms on Michigan's upper peninsula. Some states are finding that the most effective way to be comprehensive and efficient is to **organize by industrial sector**. Oklahoma, for instance, plans to organize offices for each of its major industrial sectors as part of its technology extension program.

What SMEs need is comprehensive strategic planning

Good programs are accessible to firms in communities of all sizes and in all places: Programs that operate only out of state universities or urban centers are unlikely to extend very far across large states, unless some special outreach provisions are made. Southern Arkansas University's Technical Branch operates four mobile training and demonstration vans. Georgia Tech and Minnesota Technology, Inc., operate out of regional field offices. The Mid-America Manufacturing Technology Center is retraining Kansas' cooperative extension agents to assess SMEs' problems and provide appropriate assistance. Every modernization program ought to be assessed according to how well it addresses the needs of its most remote clients. Recognizing that economies of scale may preclude the same level of services in less populated areas as in urban centers, mechanisms for overcoming access barriers are needed.

Every modernization program ought to be assessed according to how well it addresses the needs of its most remote clients

Kentucky's Community Colleges and the Center for Robotics and Manufacturing Systems: Partnerships on Wheels

In 1988, when the Southern Technology Council sought membership for its Consortium for Manufacturing Competitiveness (CMC) from the state of Kentucky, the unlikely site was Somerset Community College. It was considered risky to demonstrate the potential of the state's two-year colleges to support industrial modernization there because Somerset was located in a poor and rural area. It, along with most of the state's community college system, was oriented toward academic transfer programs, not technical degrees, and although the college had organized training programs for a few local industries, it had no industrial technology program or advanced technology laboratories in place.

In Kentucky, area vocational centers provide most of the skills training but cannot offer the technical associate degree required for CMC membership. Lacking the experience in advanced technologies, the college turned to the newly formed industrial extension program at the University of Kentucky's college of engineering for support. A "letter of partnership agreement" between the partners—the Center for Robotics and Manufacturing Systems (CRMS) Industrial Extension Service and Somerset Community College representing the Southern Technology Council—defined the purposes and terms. In essence, the 14-institution community college system agreed to assign its business and industry liaison and continuing education staff to work with CRMS, and the College of Engineering agreed to provide an industrial extension coordinator as an on-site expert to respond to referrals and make the college's initial contacts to support technology extension activities.

To compensate for the community colleges' lack of industrial technology facilities and specialized expertise while taking advantage of their close ties to businesses in the area, the University of Kentucky Community College system outfitted a van with industrial technologies. The vehicle, which was donated by the Ford Motor Company, contains computer-aided design, programmable logic controllers, and a portable CNC lathe and milling machine, with plans to expand into a flexible manufacturing cell.

The van travels on request to remote small businesses to demonstrate and train in the use of advanced technologies. The 372 Cox

Group, a 50-person family-owned firm in Gilbertsville, Kentucky, was one of its stops. The Cox Group had been designing and producing plastic and fiberglass parts using drawing boards and manual processes. Chief Executive Officer Gerald Cox asked the college to provide two-week training to see if his staff could learn AutoCAD and if the company could benefit from it. The result of the two-week session was that the company purchased hardware to support 10 CAD workstations and automated its design process.

Although the van is used primarily for customized training, according to director Clarence Johns, it often gives people ideas. Programmable logic controllers, he notes, generate the most training needs. At Madisonville Community College, Danny Koon takes the van to SMEs such as a small Siemens plant in Marion, which is situated in a county so rural there are no four-lane roads; the plant needed to retrain its workforce to build electrical components in a newly automated facility. A group of three small plastics firms—one established company and two start-up firms—used the van jointly for statistical process control training. The firms, operating as an informal network, regularly share information and travel together to visit trade shows or plant sites.

The success of the partnership between the university and the community college has altered the university's relationship with all 14 community colleges in the state. As a result of the favorable ties to Somerset Community College, CRMS has trained a business and industry liaison person at each of the state's community colleges to recognize the SMEs' problems and identify experts to solve them. Staff at Madisonville Community College helped a small firm develop a prototype impeller for a water pump on the university's stereolithography unit. As a result, the SME suggested a design change to its customer that enhanced the final product. This relationship greatly expands the resources and outreach of the effective but small industrial extension staff at the University, which, if limited to its in-house resources, could never reach a significant number of the state's more than 3,000 manufacturers. In fact, a survey in 1990 found that few SMEs (about 3 percent) used university or state resources in their modernization plans. Using the community colleges as brokers and the mobile lab for on-site training support, extension can reach every corner of the state. The single van, which can only be used to train a small number of firms, is still a limiting factor, but the university has been considering additional similar vehicles.

CONTACT:
Clarence D. Johns, Coordinator of Business and Industry Services
Community College System
University of Kentucky
113 Breckinridge Hall
Lexington, Kentucky 40506-0056
(606) 257-5653

Good programs must be sustainable: Customers must value the SMEs and be willing to share or pay for service costs or the government must be willing to make a long-term commitment to subsidies that sustain programs. All parties must understand that the benefits are important to the local economy but are not something local firms can capture; communities must also realize that SMEs yield significant social benefits. The demise of the Michigan Modernization Service (MMS) illustrates the perils of aligning an effort too closely with a governor's office. This program, widely acclaimed as one of the most effective in the nation, was based on gubernatorial fiat. It lacked legislative mandate or any long-term authorization. When a new governor took office, the program was abolished. Local technical programs that turned to MMS for support and SMEs looking for new sources of assistance found serious gaps in aid instead. Most state technology programs are created with every intention of becoming self-sufficient. Federal grants to states are predicated on the idea that state, local and private funds will replace federal funds after a specified number of years. The NIST-funded Manufacturing Technology Centers, for example, receive federal funds for six years, and in diminishing amounts. Recent grants for technology extension from NIST are for one year, after which time the state is expected to assume the costs. But state grants further assume that local and private funds will replace their investments. While some experts believe that if programs are truly market-driven, they will bring fees for services, no program has achieved complete self-suffi-ciency. Some programs are, however, able to recover part of their costs, which is a useful measure of success.

Good programs respond to and stimulate demand: This is an emerging tenet of new government programs but often a difficult one to implement. Technical special-ists are inclined to promote new practices or recommend investments before the need is evident. Even cooperative extension agents have fallen into the trap of recommend-ing mechanized equipment that went beyond farmers' needs and resulted in overinvestment and underutilized equipment. Since demand is expressed ultimately by the marketplace, the best technology programs are linked to market information and development programs. Without explicit customer requirements, such as for quicker delivery, or new market requirements, such as Europe's ISO 9000 standards, SMEs generally have little interest in new investments or practices. At the same time, the public sector bears some responsibility for being clear about how to exploit the opportunities modernization can afford SMEs. The public sector can increase SMEs' appetite for modernization by developing close personal relationships that lead to trust and mutual respect with the firms; by providing information about benchmarks and setting standards; and by assessing carefully.

The best tech-nology programs are linked to market infor-mation and development programs

Good programs complement and expand private services, not duplicate them: There is no need for services that the private sector can meet adequately. But gaps do exist in private services. For example, many consulting firms will not take on small manufacturers as clients because potential contracts may be too small to warrant the time investment, and SMEs may be unable to afford the consulting services. The public sector's respon-sibilities are to: (1) fill gaps caused by too few clients to justify a service, (2) redress inequities in access, and (3) provide services or stimulate new behaviors which benefit the region or greater society, not just a firm or community. Technology extension services in rural areas give manufacturers access to information and advice that no one else can provide. Loans to minority-owned busi-

Texas' Technology Business Development:
Blending Modernization With Community Development

The Texas Engineering Experiment Station (TEES) was created by Texas A&M University in 1914, the year Congress enacted the Smith-Lever Act supporting cooperative extension. It is one of the earliest and longest standing technology programs in the nation. It remained under the college of engineering until 1948, when it was moved into the larger Texas A&M University System as a separate state agency. Currently it has 36 divisions, employs 800 people and has a research budget of more than $40 million, a significant portion of which comes from business and industry.

TEES supplies a wealth of information and resources to SMEs, and the division that is most useful to SMEs is Technology Business Development (TBD). Created in 1986 as a service division, TBD brokers the university's and the state's expertise to firms and generally makes the plethora of TEES programs understandable to the small, rural manufacturer while extension concentrates on community-based education and training activities in areas such as local development and fire safety. TBD's revenues come from the state, its EDA grant, a NASA grant, various contracts for services with federal and state agencies, and client fees. As a result of the budget deficit, the state's portion was cut from $400,000 to $250,000 in FY 1992.

The Technology Business Center (TBC) established its own extension arm in 1989 as an economic development outreach center. One of three federal Economic Development Administration-funded (EDA), university-based centers in the state, it is the most focused on technology and has had substantial statewide impact. The eight-person TBC staff is supplemented with graduate students from the college of engineering, the business school, and the department of urban and regional planning. On average, 20 students are in the field on projects.

Clients are businesses, communities, or federal and state agencies. The city of Athens, population about 10,000, for example, invited TBD to help with a long-term economic development strategy to infuse growth into its industrial base. One of the first steps was to draw on TBD's Cross-Match program to identify the sources from which local firms were buying. The key industry, the study found, was disposable medical supplies, with significant domestic and global growth potential. A result of the project—carried out by a TBD team of two professionals, two graduate students and Athens business leaders—was to identify or establish new local suppliers for this growth market. The end result was a plan for a new business incubator to develop the capacity to manufacture supplies related to that industry; several companies were expected to relocate to Athens by the end of 1992.

In another case, three rural counties in northern Texas were convinced there was a way to increase the value added of their cotton production, 92 percent of which was being shipped out of state. There was no reason, the local cooperative extension agent asserted, that textiles could not be produced closer to home. TBD was asked to study the potential for textile production, and experts from industry and the Textile Research Center at Texas Tech evaluated the technical, financial and marketing feasibility. The region, they concluded, could set up spinning operations and ship to businesses in subsequent phases of production nearby and in east Texas.

Some of the center's business comes through contracts with other agencies such as the small business development centers. These centers provide the first level of assistance while the TBD provides the more in-depth and community-based level. The program's real strength is integrating modernization, technology transfer and utilization with local development and building a sound economic base on individual firms' improvements.

CONTACT:
Jane Mills Smith
Texas Engineering Experiment Station
Technology Business Development
Texas A&M University System
310 Wisenbaker Engineering Research Center
College Station, Texas 77843-3369
(409) 845-0538

nesses counteract the reluctance of some financial institutions to make loans to minorities with insufficient financial history. Education and generic training, for example, address the greater good of society.

Good programs involve SME owners/managers and labor in their design and planning: If SMEs are truly market-driven, they must know from the start what services firms need most and how the firms are best approached. Governments tend to have close ties to the largest businesses, and chief executive officers of large corporations frequently sit on state commissions and boards. Counterparts from small, rural firms are rarely asked to participate, but this practice is beginning to change. When the Oklahoma Center for the Advancement of Science and Technology received a federal grant in 1991 to plan a new technology extension program, it assembled a large group about equally composed of small manufacturing companies' managers from the most remote parts of the state, government officials, and vocational-technical school staff members. This group spent two days discussing and debating the needs of small firms, the services that would be most useful to the firms and appropriate delivery systems. At the meeting's conclusion, a task force was named with considerable private sector representation to continue the planning process. Oregon's Wood Products Competitiveness Corporation, a modernization initiative enacted by the legislature in 1991, was designed only after numerous meetings and discussions with industry representatives. Labor involvement in program planning and design is less commonplace in the United States than it is in Europe. Northern industrial states are more likely to include union representatives than other states, a reflection of the low rate of unionization among small and rural firms in areas outside the Rust Belt.

Good programs improve a region's level of skills and wages and quality of work life: Small and medium-sized manufacturers in the United States typically pay low wages and provide poor benefits. Convincing SMEs that competitiveness depends on a skilled, innovative and contented workforce is perhaps the most challenging aspect of rural industrial modernization. Minnesota Technology Inc., and the Tri-State Manufacturers Association help small firms understand and reward the value of skills. COSMOS, Inc., a small metal fabricating firm in

Pennsylvania's Industrial Resource Centers: Eight Points of Light

In 1988, the Pennsylvania Department of Commerce established nine industrial resource centers (IRCs) as non-profit corporations managed and operated by private industry but supported by the commonwealth. (In 1992, two IRCs were consolidated into one.) Each was given the mission of helping small and medium-sized manufacturers, both individually and collectively, learn about and adopt new production technologies, techniques and philosophies in ways that respond to total business needs. Each IRC had considerable leeway in how it was organized, administered, governed and chose to work with firms.

IRCs can establish specialized centers to provide knowledge directly, but mainly they exist to provide information and conduct free or low-cost technology audits and assessments and identify and support implementation projects. As independent businesses, they can charge for services and, in fact, are expected to work toward that goal. For IRC services, they generally pay a rate based on the field agent's salary. Once needs are identified, staff are much more likely to match firms with resources, consultants or services than to address needs themselves. The IRC usually subsidizes about 25 percent of the fees of consultants or services up to $6,500 per project.

The Northwest Pennsylvania Industrial Resource Center (NPIRC) reaches from its home port of Erie into 13 primarily rural counties to help modernize the 2,000 manufacturers based there. Given the large territory, NPIRC has opened an outreach office at Clarion University, about 90 miles south of Erie. This office focuses on powdered metals and related industries. The IRC is governed by a board that consists of three representatives of each member of the coalition it formed. Members include two local universities, two economic development agencies, the manufacturers' association, the chamber of commerce and the National Institute of Flexible Manufacturing.

With a staff of only three professionals, including one in Clarion, and an annual budget of $720,000, the NPIRC director must leverage whatever services are available. For instance, NPIRC has an agreement with the Great Lakes Manufacturing Technology Center (MTC) in Cleveland, Ohio (one of NIST's five regional centers) to become an outreach center. The MTC supplements NPIRC's expertise in a variety of ways. For example, two-person teams from MTC and NPIRC assessed 16 firms' needs and opportunities to modernize over the nine months of the cooperative agreement. Upon completion, the team made a personal presentation to management and provided a written report. For the service, NPIRC paid MTC $1,000, or half of the assessment's estimated cost. The IRC also depends on the MTC in Cleveland for "Rural Manufacturing Outreach Programs," which are demonstrations of new processes developed by NIST's MTC and called the "Shop of the '90s." The first program was offered in Meadville, Pennsylvania, in mid-1991.

NPIRC also is exploring working relationships with the NASA Industrial Applications Center in Pittsburgh and the Pennsylvania Technical Assistance Program (PENNTAP) at Penn State University. Through a grant from the Appalachian Regional Commission, the IRC is working with the Northwest Commission's Revolving Loan Fund, conducting an "ailing business" project. The project conducts assessments, prepares analyses and recommendations, and recommends consultants to assist the firm; the funds can be used to pay the remaining 75 percent of the costs not covered by NPIRC. In 1991, 26 firms benefitted from the grant.

Two other unusual and innovative NPIRC projects are the Manufacturing and Innovation Networks Initiative (MAIN) and the National Institute of Flexible Manufacturing. MAIN was designed to strengthen the region's plastics industry through alliances. It has four target areas: marketing, education, technology and labor management. In its early years, the alliance formed committees to seek solutions and compiled a directory of its capabilities to market the region; began trade negotiations with Canada; disseminated a standardized testing procedure; began developing an associate degree program in plastic engineering technology at Penn State's Erie campus; developed tooling and machining/moldmaking training programs; established a mold debugging capability at the Plastics Technology Center at Penn State in Erie; and collaborated with two universities outside the state to develop new technologies.

The National Institute of Flexible Manufacturing (NIFM) is an ambitious attempt, sparked initially by the U.S. Department of Commerce's interest in assessing the market for a shared manufacturing training and demonstration center. After a slow start, NIFM managed to acquire six CNC machines. By mid-1992, 50 firmq had used the facility, and about 15 firms were sharing it. In 1991, NIFM linked up with Gannon University to participate in the IBM CIM/ Higher Education Partnership, preparing the university to teach Computer-Integrated Manufacturing. NPIRC Director David Anderson believes this shared advanced facilities concept is the wave of the future for rural areas. He expects to "clone" NIFM in two or three rural locations, providing manufacturers with access to equipment they could not otherwise afford. Vendors, he notes, are more than willing to share the equipment costs as demonstrations of their latest equipment.

Through this array of programs, NPIRC, between its inception in 1988 and June 30, 1991, reached 264 firms. Of that total, 114 had 25 or fewer employees and only 27 had more than 150 employees. About 60 percent were from non-metropolitan counties. The most common services, which account for more than half the projects, have been market expansion and technology improvement, manufacturing strategies, and production planning and inventory control. All of the IRCs are evaluated yearly and funded according to availability of funds and evaluation results. In an effort to reach more firms through group services, the evaluation criteria were revised in 1990 so that 30 percent of the evaluation was based on networking or collective activities.

Interest in helping NPIRC is growing as it becomes better known and trusted by SMEs, according to Anderson. But at the same time, its state allocation has been reduced—which was anticipated as IRCs replaced state funds with revenues generated from projects, fees for services and other sources. NPIRC's funding from the state, for instance, was 21.5 percent lower in 1991–92 than the previous year. Because of increased demand, by six months into the fiscal year, IRC had met its annual goal of 60 projects but had little funding left for additional projects.

CONTACT:
Robert W. Coy, Jr., Director, Office of Technology Development
Pennsylvania Department of Commerce
352 Forum Building
Harrisburg, Pennsylvania 17120
(717) 787-4147

rural Minnesota, and an active member of the Tri-State Manufacturers Association, allows its employees to develop their ideas into new products or processes and to file patents; COSMOS keeps all employees in some capacity, even during slow seasons. As a result, the firm is able to stay on the cutting edge of its industry. State practices that encourage and reward such policies, however, are difficult to find.

Good programs feature a return on investment mentality: This approach attempts to maximize the value of public sector investments and promotes a focus on identifying program clients, producing practical results, and discouraging a preoccupation with internal process. Individuals and programs infused with this mindset must consider day-to-day choices constantly in light of short- versus long-term strategies, risk versus return tradeoffs. Just as important, this approach promotes a culture in which program personnel think and behave like their private sector constituents. It is not an argument for calculating returns precisely but merely as a tool for discussing costs, intended and actual results, and relative value. There is an important distinction to be made, however, between calculating returns from public programs and those from private firms. The public sector can, and in fact ought to, place values on social outcomes and consider how its actions affect various populations and places. Investment returns to targeted disadvantaged populations or distressed areas, for instance, must be considered in light of the value to the state and society, as well as to the client firms.

Current State Efforts

Spurred by OEMs' greater emphasis on and higher expectations of their suppliers, states finally are beginning to focus on the SMEs' needs. Some states have, in the past five years, established programs and allocated modest levels of resources aimed at modernization. A survey of state and federal technology extension programs (all programs providing direct services aimed at

State finally are beginning to focus on the SME's needs

transferring technology, modernizing processes, and improving productivity and profitability) was conducted in 1989 by the National Governors' Association (NGA) with the assistance of National Institute of Standards and Technology. The study identified programs to assist SMEs with modernization in only 13 states and found that these programs accounted for only 4 percent of all expenditures reported in the survey. NGA's recommendations encouraged states and the federal government to increase their emphasis on **improving and diffusing proven manufacturing technologies** and called on the federal government to catalyze, support, research, and record such activities. Federal interest has indeed increased, accompanied by modest levels of support, and it has led to expanded activities. The sum total of services, however, still is clearly insufficient for the task at hand.

State programs and policies to modernize manufacturing in rural areas use **seven strategies**: brokering services, providing information, assessing needs, solving problems, demonstrating new technologies or techniques, providing support services and offering incentives. Most programs, however, are hybrids, employing more than one strategy. For example, centers do some outreach, brokers provide information, and support services may be linked to incentives. Thus the examples cited are not intended to compartmentalize a particular program. Each strategy employs some mix of: (1) collective action; (2) one-on-one assistance; (3) general support services; (4) information systems; and (5) system and infrastructure to achieve its goals.

Strategy One—State programs provide brokering services: Programs match SME problems or needs with experts who have solutions or services. The effective broker is able to quickly assess a situation, identify the real problem or need, then find an individual, company, or public agency that can respond. It is important that **brokers be generalists** so that they do not arrive with a portfolio of technical solutions in search of a problem but can, instead, consider the full range of business functions from market exploration through delivery to customer. Maryland's Office of Technology Development expects the directors of its six regional technology councils to identify brokers. Not specialists, council directors are expected to work with others to coordinate needs, facilitate cooperation, and make sure SME needs are met. Pennsylvania's Industrial Resource Centers also view the principal role of their staffs as that of brokers, utilizing existing public and private resources to avoid duplication of services or competition with private sector services. The field staff of Minnesota Technology, Inc., is one step closer to the firms, helping them to assess their needs but not solving their problems.

Strategy Two—States provide information: Programs collect the information directly through their educational activities. Information, for example, about economic conditions and markets collected by the public sector and information basic to the vitality of an industry sector but too expensive for individual firms to compile needs to be made **equally accessible** to firms of all sizes and in all communities. Cooperative extension is the most renowned example of this information exchange: county agents provide agriculture-related information to farmers, suppliers, processors, and consumers via pamphlets, seminars and, more recently, information systems.

No state has yet replicated cooperative extension's information transfer attributes in the industrial sector, although there have been some recent efforts. Several northeastern states, under the auspices of the Northeast Manufacturing Technology Center, have created TECnet at Tufts University. TECnet is a database for SMEs that includes, among other things, information about government regulations and programs, requests by large firms for bids, listings of used equipment for sale, information about import-export, and training opportunities. The Oklahoma Center for the Advancement for Science and Technology (OCAST) offers free searches to SMEs on the Technical Resources Access Center (TRAC), a database OCAST maintains of consultants and experts in the state's universities. Minnesota Project Outreach (MPO) is a program designed to provide free information to rural firms with less than $10 million in annual revenues. MPO will provide a database of expert advice,

TECnet is a database for SMEs

market information, and literature searches through the services of TelTech, a private firm with NIST funding that is demonstrating its ability to serve small Minnesota businesses. In Kentucky, community-based telework centers are planned. Based on successful models in Scandinavia, telework centers in rural locations will make the latest telecommunications information available to everyone in the vicinity. Information can also be provided more directly, through continuing education programs of universities or colleges. Increasingly, colleges and private companies are offering seminars and workshops in various new management technologies and approaches to business decisions at remote locations across the states.

Strategy Three—State programs assess technology needs and help identify problems: Without minimizing the importance of responding to market demand, there is a need to stimulate demand. Frequently the managers of small and rural firms fail to recognize underlying problems. When the University of Tennessee asked 26 firms if they had any pressing problems, not one responded that it did. Yet when the university visited the firms and closely examined their production processes, every one had a major production problem to be solved. Minnesota Technology, Inc., staff have found that by beginning with perceived problems, which may be only symptoms of more serious shortcomings, they can help businesses understand more fundamental needs. Michigan's Industrial Technology Institute has developed a tool to help assess technology needs called TAP, which has been adopted by a variety of states and Canadian provinces. Each of these tools, however, can only supplement, not substitute for, the skilled analyst.

Strategy Four—State programs help firms solve technical problems involving products, production process, system integration or management: It is a common approach among industrial extension services for a program to offer limited technical assistance, expecting the client to pay for services beyond an introductory phase. The earliest of such programs, industrial extension at North Carolina State and Georgia Tech and PENNTAP

Minnesota Technology, Inc.: Reaching Out, Rebuilding Confidence

Thief River Falls, Minnesota, population 9,000, does not seem like the kind of place you would find a technology center, but Jim Lambert directs one there out of his satellite office. Headquartered in Moorhead just a few minutes from the North Dakota border, Lambert and three other professional staff deliver services for Minnesota Technology, Inc., to manufacturers in 22 northwestern Minnesota counties. The far-flung staff of this regional outpost are located in Moorhead, Detroit Lakes, Alexandria and Thief River Falls—a rural territory that spans an area 300 miles by 150 miles.

The goals of Lambert's program are clearly defined as providing SMEs with the knowledge to identify their needs—particularly for off-the-shelf technologies, modern management methods, and training—and to help them use these tools to improve production capabilities, efficiency and product quality. His staff is not expected to solve problems; instead, they help business managers think about where they want to be in three to five years and what they need to be competitive, then identify what it will take to get them there. If the firm requires consultants or other external services, Minnesota Technology is authorized to subsidize up to half the costs—if there is a long-term commitment to modernization. Lambert and his staff also look for opportunities to form industry consortia or networks that might make the firms more competitive internationally. Every visit must be carefully documented for accountability and evidence of impact.

Building the firms' trust and gaining their confidence is a slow process. In the three months between July 1 and October 1, 1991, Lambert and his staff visited 50 firms—most with fewer than 50 employees—and identified 46 distinct projects. They frequently find that the problem they are asked to address is not the real problem, and their challenge is convincing the firm's owner to focus on the underlying problems, not just the symptoms. Despite the fact that Lambert and his staff can, in theory, call on outside experts, they are so far from the centers of engineering resources that they are forced to be quite resourceful themselves. Although there are two Minnesota state colleges and technical schools in the area, the University of North Dakota and North Dakota State University are the closest sources of concentrated expertise. In fact, Lambert hopes that sometime soon his staff might be able to serve, on a fee basis, manufacturers across the state lines.

With firms so far apart, travel consumes a great deal of staff time to spread the word about Minnesota Technology services. Therefore, they use every occasion to address groups, including Rotary clubs, chambers of commerce, and other civic organizations. One of the potentially valuable groups is the Tri-State Manufacturers Association, formed in 1989 and the recipient of a grant from the Northwest Area Foundation to act as a catalyst for manufacturing networks. At least one of Lambert's staff members attends each monthly association meeting. Lambert thinks that the network concept is a great opportunity; developing networks among companies in the area is one of his goals.

Most of the manufacturers in the region, according to Lambert, have made little use of automation—often not even desktop computers for accounting. One of the most promising and innovative of his projects—a form of collaboration among small firms and a local electric company—attempts to introduce computer systems. With excess capacity on its computer for Materials Resource Planning (MRP), the utility company is willing to lease time via modems to SMEs. The SME saves the cost of hardware and software and must invest only in training. If successful, Lambert hopes to establish an "MRP incubator" in which firms can use the utilities' equipment for 12 to 18 months to test the system's value before investing money in it. Lambert has discovered that many of the firms he visits need market information before considering modernization. This falls under the mission of Minnesota Technology only if the information becomes part of a firm's long-term strategy. If the firm simply wants marketing assistance, the staff will suggest faculty or graduate students at nearby colleges or other resources to help.

This statewide program of Minnesota Technology is the progeny of another, not-so-successful attempt to apply technology to rural development. The Rural Development Act of 1987 established the Greater Minnesota Corporation (GMC) and appropriated $95.5 million as an endowment, expecting the corporation to operate using the interest. This act, according to a principal author, Senator Roger Moe, was to allow local communities to take more control over their own development and to direct companies and entrepreneurs seeking technical assistance to R&D specialists or technical colleges who could help them. It authorized four regional research institutes, an agricultural utilization research institute, and financial assistance programs. In 1988, the Minnesota legislature rescinded most of the corporation's funds in exchange for a portion of the proceeds from the state's lottery.

In an effort to develop local ownership, GMC created a number of separate, non-profit organizations around the state. Each organization developed its own programs, but also had its own agenda, constituents, boards, and programs. There was little strategic thought given to how all of these programs would be coordinated and related to other state programs. Financial and administrative mismanagement, disparate elements and charges of an urban bias brought the GMC to a crisis point in 1990. The legislature recaptured most of the start-up funds, leaving only $12 million for operations. GMC's options were to disband or reorganize. The state took the latter road and hired as its new president Jacques Koppel, a nationally known and highly respected administrator with considerable experience in Pennsylvania. In his first year in office, working hard to regain the confidence of the legislature, Koppel reorganized the state's program under a new entity—Minnesota Technology, Inc.

The new organization made sure that it addressed the needs of rural businesses. While continuing to support various research institutes, other organizations and a new pilot database—Minnesota Project Outreach—Minnesota Technology consolidated many GMC functions into a set of comprehensive services. The new streamlined services are delivered through six offices. With all overhead functions centralized at the single home office, the five regional centers are able to concentrate exclusively on services outside the seven-county metropolitan areas for SMEs and entrepreneurs. Jim Lambert's region is part of Koppel's new vision.

CONTACT:
Jacques Koppel, President
Minnesota Technology, Inc.
920 Second Avenue South, Suite 1250
Minneapolis, Minnesota 55402
(612) 338-7722

Indiana's Regional Technology Councils: Building Hubs

Indiana is part of what has become known as the Rust Belt, the nation's oldest manufacturing region. Hit hard by the recession of 1979–82, the region began an intensive modernization campaign to make its manufacturing base competitive once again. The Corporation for Science and Technology (CST) was established in 1982 to invest in R&D by young and start-up companies and to establish technology transfer offices at two university-based service centers. In 1991, as the state refocused on its traditional industry base, the mission expanded to help small manufacturers upgrade their operations. To emphasize the importance of this task, CST changed its name to the Indiana Business Modernization and Technology Corporation (BMTC).

Citing evidence of declining competitiveness of the nation's industry (similar to that mentioned previously in this book), Indiana embarked on a pilot Manufacturing Technology Service Program in 1989. During the first year of operation, the corporation created five regional centers, each directed by a person with industrial experience. These centers operate as tax-exempt, non-profit hub organizations, always co-located with other business services such as the chambers of commerce, Small Business Development Centers, SCORE, incubators, or financial assistance offices.

The design calls for a market-driven, pro-active process to reach SMEs, one flexible enough to accommodate regional differences and innovative approaches. It also recognizes the importance of facilitating interfirm collaboration, both among agencies that provide services and among firms themselves. The model, according to program Director Bob Bassler, is the center as "hub," the function-specific support agencies as "spokes," and the center director as "scout," who assesses SME needs and finds resources to help. "This approach," he says, "avoids unnecessary duplication of administrative support and lets the center directors focus on what they know best, delivery of services." In addition to finding resources, directors look for ways firms can interact with each other, and one of the centers' evaluation criteria is identifying opportunities to build networks. The pilot resulted in sufficient success to expand to 10 centers statewide in late 1991; there has been some discussion about adding four more.

Expectations for the centers are high in comparison with the corporation's funding ($50,000 per center with a 50 percent local match required from the public and/or private sectors), based on leveraging other resources such as in-kind services or through other programs. The way the centers can achieve substantial impact is by calling on other state programs with funding to provide in-depth support, such as Purdue's Technical Assistance Program, Indiana University's Industrial Research Liaison Program or Infonet, Indiana State's Technical Service Center, the University of Southern Indiana Technical Service Center, Small Business Development Centers, and Cooperative Extension Service, acting as liaison between the firms and these support services. If the technical demand is beyond the mission of public sector organizations, the centers will suggest private consultants and, on request, help the firms evaluate their proposals. One region adopted the Manufacturing Network Program, based on the experiences in northern Italy and Denmark, to assemble groups of manufacturers to work on common problems.

The state has made a long-term commitment to the project and, although local funding is stable, has expanded the number of centers and the core support from the corporation. But even drawing on state resources and using networks to achieve economies of scale, the investment is low. To expand to a scale to have a significant impact on the nearly 5,000 SMEs in the state, centers may need to charge for their services in the future.

CONTACT:
Robert B. Bassler, Director, Manufacturing Technology Services
Indiana Corporation for Science and Technology
One North Capitol Avenue, Suite 925
Indianapolis, Indiana 46204-2242
(317) 635-3058

at Pennsylvania State University, called on professional staff in their colleges of engineering to help firms with technical production, design or productivity problems. How effective these programs are in rural areas depends in large part on how widely the staff is dispersed. Georgia Tech's program is highly decentralized, with 12 field offices across the state. The Michigan Modernization Service employed consultants to address SMEs' problems.

How effective these programs are in rural areas depends in large part on how widely the staff is dispersed

Even programs that address problems directly are careful to limit their advice so as not to compete with the private sector or to give some firms unfair advantage. (PENNTAP is quick to claim that it is not a consulting service, calling itself instead a disseminator of information.) Most state programs, in fact, limit the number of days per firm and average only two to three days per client.

Still another mechanism for solving problem and providing technical assistance is the Small Business Administration's **Small Business Development Centers**. In theory, these centers represent a significant resource for SMEs, but in practice—with only a few notable exceptions—they tend to focus on business start-up problems and are not staffed by people with industrial expertise. One exception is the North Carolina Small Business and Technology Development Center, which employs some field staff with manufacturing experience and reached about 600 manufacturers with some form of service in 1990.

Strategy Five—State programs demonstrate new technologies or techniques: At the same time, they establish models and conduct research and development that is available to SMEs. Generally, centers are either technology-specific, such as the Center for Robotics and Manufacturing Systems at the University of Kentucky and the shared flexible manufacturing facility at Hagerstown Junior College in Maryland, or industry-specific, such as the textile centers at Clemson and Auburn Universities or the furniture production technology center at Itawamba Community College in Mississippi. These programs have state-of-the-art technology and are open to firms that want to observe or test new processes or build prototypes.

Early demonstration centers located at universities, modeled after agricultural experiment stations, were called **industrial experiment stations**, such as the industrial experiment station at Texas A&M. Georgia Tech's engineering experiment station was reorganized with an expanded mission and renamed the Georgia Tech Research Institute. More recently, driven by an increasing demand for quality, centers for industrial quality assurance have become popular, as illustrated by the University

Georgia Tech: The Granddaddy of Extension

Georgia passed legislation in 1959 (Code Chapter 32-2, No. 909) that created the Georgia Institute of Technology—a central engineering experiment station, field offices or "substations," and an industrial development center. Its purposes were "to encourage further industrial and economic development" and "to provide an industrial extension service to meet the needs of industry and local development groups." Field offices were established at seven cities between 1961 and 1966, and five were added later.

The Engineering Experiment Station eventually became know as the Georgia Tech Research Institute (GTRI), which administers the Economic Development Laboratory (EDL) and 19 other laboratories. Industrial Extension Service is one of several campus-based technology outreach programs under EDL. According to the legislation, clients could be firms or local development organizations. GTRI would compile economic data, conduct seminars, and—a major task during the early years—help recruit businesses to the state. In the mid-1980s, the six regional offices of the extension service were expanded and re-named Georgia Technology Centers.

Regional offices, staffed by one engineer and a secretary, are too small to work directly with firms on specific problems so extension engineers must limit their time with a given firm to five days, after which the firm must contract with Georgia Tech or a consultant. According to GTRI Director David Clifton, "Our engineers can answer about 70 percent of the questions they get; for the rest they call in outside experts." These experts come from the other GTRI laboratories, other EDL technology outreach programs, as well as from other schools in the state. Experts from the Apparel Manufacturing Technology Center, the hazardous waste assistance program, the agricultural Technology Program, and the Economic Development Administration's University Centers have been involved in this way with GTRI. Each center supplements its services through the college's cooperative student program, drawing on undergraduate and graduate students to work on industrial problems and putting students to work directly in manufacturing companies. In mid-1992, there were more than 1,000 co-op students working in Georgia.

In 1984–85, more than 1,200 businesses, 96 percent of which had fewer than 250 employees, contacted the extension service. In 1990, GTRI counted 2,110 contacts, half of which requested information, nearly 300 wanted in-plant training, and 200 asked for direct technical assistance. The operating budget for FY 1991 included $4.3 million of state funds (excluding overhead) and $4.2 of federal funds, most of which was for an Apparel Manufacturing Technology Center funded by the U.S. Department of Defense. The Industrial Extension Service's budget was $3 million in state funds, and a small one-year grant from NIST in FY 1991 to demonstrate alternative forms of technology deployment, including mass mailings, videos and one-day conferences. To measure its impact, the program requests that each client evaluate benefits and results. The evaluation form asks about degree of satisfaction with the consultation and anticipated outcomes, such as savings, jobs saved or created, increased sales, intent to implement, estimated investment, and time in person-days the client spends implementing recommendations.

The key to the program's success is its outreach, conducted through the regional centers. The office in Douglas, population 13,000, for example, is under the direction of Sherman Dudley and serves 17 rural counties in south-central Georgia. Past president of the Georgia Industrial Developers Association, he also manages the six regional offices in the southern half of the state. To reach manufacturers and generate demand for their services, the field offices use existing organizations. Dudley, for example, spoke to seven of his region's nine industry committees in 1991.

In that same year, Dudley's office handled 63 technical assistance projects and assisted with 25 economic development projects. Examples of assistance include providing a plant layout and feasibility study for a machinery firm moving to Baxley; helping a marine windshield manufacturer in Nashville evaluate new process changes in its cutting operation; and, in cooperation with a chemistry professor from Georgia Tech, helping a company in Douglas develop a technology to mass produce a chemical compound that removes cesium from radioactive waste.

Client evaluations testify to the services' value. A Georgia Tech Extension engineer, for instance, helped a 25-person firm install a computer system and analyze the company's entire operation. The CEO of Recordex Corp., wrote that "without Georgia Tech's help, Recordex would be in liquidation today, but instead its successor, Recordex Manufacturing is a going concern." The CEO of Volumatic, Inc., wrote that Georgia Tech "expanded our view of where we have to go." Still another engineer helped Samsom Industries develop automated welding machines and leak testing procedures, which the CEO estimated saved the firm $10,000.

Field engineers throughout the state call on each other for their special expertise. An engineer in Savannah knows marketing and is called to handle market information, and the engineer in Albany knows the agricultural equipment sectors. Each field office also is able to access computer database searches, providing quick information on a wide variety of subjects.

Even at Georgia Tech, one of the largest state extension programs in the nation, there clearly are not enough staff to handle demand. The Douglas office ended 1991 with a backlog of 23 projects, which forced staff to be more reactive and less proactive than they would like. Due to state budget deficits that year, the program's funding was cut nearly 7 percent.

Georgia Tech's Research Institute is clearly a valuable resource for the state and has operated as a de facto science and technology policy arm of state government since Georgia is one of a small number of states without a state science and technology agency or office. Its strengths are a dispersed staff, a strong college of engineering to provide backup and a track record that extends over three decades.

CONTACT:
David Swanson, Director
Georgia Tech Research Institute
Georgia Institute of Technology
Economic Development Laboratory
Atlanta, Georgia 30332
(404) 894-6100

of Maryland's Center for Quality and Productivity and the University of North Carolina's Center for Industrial Quality Assurance at Charlotte. Two-year colleges— which tend to be more accessible in rural areas, more apt to have technologies closer to SME needs and perhaps characterized by a less threatening environment—may be the most appropriate sites for demonstration centers. Fifteen colleges with exceptionally strong industrial programs and resources are currently participating in the Consortium for Manufacturing Competitiveness, a project trying to build resource centers that can take SMEs a step or two beyond their current status. Some centers overcome spatial problems by making their facilities transportable, by putting expert systems on wheels; Arkansas and Kentucky have mobile demonstration and training facilities, and Kansas had one on the drawing boards in mid-1992.

Strategy Six—State programs provide direct support services: While services can include training, export assistance, financial assistance, and strategic planning, training is the most common support offered. It is generally carried out through two-year colleges, continuing education divisions of universities or colleges, or area vocational centers. Training that is tailored to a company's specific organization and processes is the best-known example of direct support. Most states make customized training readily available in rural areas through local educational institutions, but have designed it as an incentive to recruit branch plants, not to help SMEs modernize. A few states have established programs, such as North Carolina's Focused Industry Training (FIT), explicitly for smaller firms, but few manufacturers' needs are being met. Public financial assistance, unless associated with a new product or plant expansion, also is rare. Most state funds are for seed or venture capital, not for improving manufacturing processes, and aimed at high-risk, high-growth companies. Some states have tax incentives for SMEs and branch plants to encourage investments in new technologies. South Carolina offers firms sales and use tax exemptions for production machinery, repair parts, in-process inventory, and fuel and electricity used for manufacturing.

A few states have established programs explicitly for smaller firms

Strategy Seven—State agencies provide incentives to innovate, expand markets, and modernize: Vouchers, grants and tax deductions or credits are examples of incentives. Oregon, for example, enacted legislation for its

Northern Economic Initiatives Center: One-Stop Shopping

Michigan's Upper Peninsula is rural and far more accessible to Canada than to the United States closest major city is eight hours away by car. The peninsula's economy depends heavily on government employment and transfer payments. Private sector employment historically has been in mining and forestry-related businesses, although there are growing numbers of wood- and metal product-producing firms. The isolation of firms from their markets, from research and development, and from technical resources, including product certification and testing, has made it difficult for them to stay up to date with the newest production methods and management practices. Universities have been seen as academic institutions and not of practical value to traditional manufacturers.

Five years ago, Northern Michigan University, located in Marquette on the southern shore of Lake Superior, established the Northern Economic Initiatives Center (NEIC) to improve its relationships with local businesses. The university's position from the start was that it was an incubator; it was intended was to spin off as a self-standing center shortly after its start. In April 1992, NEIC, which then had 12 full-time staff members, became an independent, tax-exempt non-profit corporation. It maintains its ties to the university, however, employing student interns and holding training sessions on campus. About one-third of its funding comes from the state through the university, and this will continue. Most of the rest comes from foundation grants. Only about 5 to 10 percent is raised through workshops, fees and sales of materials. NEIC is looking at ways to increase revenue generated from industrial network services, but that is likely to happen in the distant future.

NEIC began operations with management training, education and counseling by housing the Small Business Development Center, and, with other development agencies in the area, took on a wide range of activities. NEIC is organized into two divisions—Industry Innovation and Alliances and the Small Business Development Center, which houses an industrial extension service. The real emphasis has been on basic industries, ones that could export or replace imports. NEIC decided it would focus about 80 percent of its efforts on the industries with the most potential for growth: secondary wood products, food processing, artisan crafts, and metal fabrication. The remaining 20 percent is for other manufacturers and service industries.

Until 1991, NEIC hosted the Michigan Modernization Service (MMS) and was able to have an engineer operating out of Marquette. With the demise of the MMS program, NEIC devised a unique industrial extension program with the help of a Michigan foundation. It features an in-house case manager, who coordinates the delivery of private sector services to firms facing engineering, operations management or cost accounting issues. Through this program, NEIC has established a relationship with Michigan Tech in Houghton (the nation's fourteenth largest engineering school) to be able to call on its technical faculty.

To help businesses overcome the high costs associated with their rural isolation, NEIC's staff turned to the concept of manufacturing networks. Industry Innovation and Alliances Director Bonnie Holland, for example, has worked with wood shops with 5 to 20 employees and the peninsula's five larger furniture products employers, who employ between 100 and 300 employees. She's trying to help the smaller firms modernize—including assessing their computer needs, jointly ordering equipment and offering training—to qualify them as subcontractors to the larger firms. The five larger firms, whose operations span about 50 miles, already meet regularly, tour each other's plants and collaborate on activities. NEIC has brought them together to learn about activity-based cost accounting and state procedures to obtain clean air and clean water permits. Requiring marketing advice that is not readily available in the region, the larger SMEs jointly met with two experts from Atlanta to learn what they had to offer. Each time the firms meet, new forms of sharing take place. One firm that had adopted the materials resource program, MRP II, offered to help another firm implement it. Others, addressing common transportation problems, entered into a five-year partnership with the Industry Technology Institute/Midwest Manufacturing Technology Center of Ann Arbor to fund joint continuous improvement projects. Five of the smaller firms have joined together to produce and market a coordinated furniture line. The aim is to evolve a private sector-supported and -staffed manufacturing network.

While the secondary wood sector is the farthest along in networking activities, other sectors are showing evidence of efforts to form networks. Thirty-five maple syrup processors have published grading standards, inspected their syrup collectively and are selling bulk syrup wholesale. In Delta County, a group of metal fabricating firms have formed a manufacturing group to identify needs they might address collectively. The catalyst was the Escanaba city manager who had learned of the NEIC furniture networks and asked both the local community college and NEIC to help organize nearby firms. Still in its early stages, early meetings indicate substantial promise.

Two other needs are driving new NEIC initiatives. The first is the lack of industrial design capacity among manufacturing. One of the major deficiencies of American manufacturing, according to many critics, is its inability to use design competitively. With no independent industrial designers on the peninsula, manufacturers are forced to ignore the issue or develop local talents. NEIC organized a group of local educators to join a tour of European design programs. This resulted in a plan to incorporate industrial design into high schools' and colleges' technical curricula, making design an integral part of technical education, as it is in many parts of Europe. NEIC is beginning the process by placing industrial design students in manufacturing plants as apprentices, counseling firms directly, and focusing on design as a competitive tool in industrial symposia. In addition, it is placing "artists-in-residence" in other manufacturing plants for two to three weeks.

Capital is the other barrier to modernization that NEIC is addressing. With local banks unwilling and unable to provide venture capital or to take risks with expansions of new technologies, NEIC is becoming an affiliate of the Shorebank Corporation (a development bank in Chicago). By June 1992 Shorebank was expected to open a loan production office and operate North Coast BIDCO, which will be able to make development loans to business.

NEIC understands that network activities provide a more immediate impact within an industry sector only by continuing to improve the competitive position of each individual firm. Services are balanced, therefore, to act as catalysts for change in individual firms, resulting in systemic change within diverse industries.

CONTACT:
H. Richard Anderson, Director
Northern Economic Initiatives Center
Northern Michigan University
1009 West Ridge Street
Marquette, Michigan 49855
(906) 227-2406

wood products industry in 1991 that provides both challenge grant funds for innovative and collective activities that must be matched and service vouchers as a partial rebate for the purchase of services essential to modernization. The Illinois Department of Commerce requested proposals to help SMEs establish networks for entering export markets. Although the objective is clearly to export, brokers will help firms with a range of joint activities, including product development, manufacturing and services. In 1989, the now defunct Michigan Modernization Service competitively awarded 17 grants of up to $25,000 for collective services linked to modernization, some of which were made to networks in rural areas.

Chapter 3. Expanding the Options for Rural Manufacturers

Most state modernization efforts are still evolving, trying to find the formulas that works best for the state's industries, labor forces and settlement patterns. Regional differences and attitudes toward economic development influence the direction and pace of change. Southern states generally are more concerned about skill levels and skilled labor market shortages, western states about distances and reaching remote firms, and northern states about high costs. Some **common themes** do seem to be occurring across regions, many ostensibly borrowed from European experiences. But, in fact, most have roots in 19th Century America and were lost in the emergence of the large, vertically integrated corporation. Others are modeled on the success of agricultural innovations and modernization.

Most state modernization efforts are still evolving

Interfirm/Multi-firm Initiatives

Among the most obvious problems facing SMEs is the inability to spread investments, expenses and risks over a wide enough production base. Consolidation has mitigated diseconomies of scale, basic to small organizations. Whether the organizations were schools, government agencies or businesses, small units have been urged to merge. But **consolidation involves tradeoffs**. Large, consolidated schools lose the ability to respond to students' and families' special needs, large governments become bureaucratic, and large businesses lose the ability to respond to customer and market changes quickly and to innovate.

In the mid-1980s, America began to note that much of its competition was coming from small, flexible enterprises in Europe and Japan that were operating in high-skill, high-wage economies, not from large, multi-national corporations operating in low-wage developing countries. U.S. competitors had recaptured the best features of community spirit with small, internally competing members pulling together to collectively face external threats and opportunities. Hundreds of these SMEs produced European furniture, apparel and machine tools; Japanese electronics, while carrying the name of large corporations, depended on independent but tightly linked SME supplier firms.

The epitome of small, modern, flexible manufacturing economy is northern Italy

The epitome of the small, modern, flexible manufacturing economy is northern Italy, lionized by Charles Sabel and Michael Piore in their widely cited book, *The Second Industrial Divide*. Built on the foundation of artisan firms, Emilia-Romagna, a region of slightly more than 4 million people that is the heart of what is now called Third Italy, pulled itself up from last in per capita income in Italy to second in two decades on the strength of its industry—more than 40,000 manufacturers that produce high-quality knitwear, ceramic tile, agricultural equipment, machinery, and other traditional products. Much of the region's success can be attributed to **interfirm linkages and collective services** provided by government, trade associations and unions, which allow small firms to use the most advanced production methods and respond quickly to the demands of global markets. Similar successes have been forged in western Germany and Sweden, where industries composed primarily of small, independently owned firms are serious players in global economies and vital parts of national economies.

The success of northern Italy's manufacturing sectors proved that SMEs working together can compete internationally on the basis of quality, design and delivery. Denmark was the first nation to introduce manufacturing networks as a national industrial policy, when the Minister of Trade and Industry announced a program to stimulate manufacturing networks throughout the nation in 1989. The program consisted of publicity and information, broker selection and training, incentives for collaboration among three or more firms, and assessment. The limited-duration program was intended to change small manufacturers' behavior and strengthen their position in European markets. Thus, Denmark became the first test of whether economic behavior that some observers suspected was culture-bound, could be transplanted in another culture. Businesses at first warned that such cooperation would never be acceptable to Danish firms and their trade associations. But, based on the experiences of the first two years, it can be and has been a successful experiment (see "Interesting Ideas From Europe," page 70). What would happen if similar policies were introduced in rural America?

As a result of small manufacturing sectors' successes in Europe and Japan, interfirm cooperation has become one of the most widely discussed new concepts in rural industrial development. Rural manufacturers in states as diverse as Oregon, Arkansas, North Carolina and Florida are creating **new alliances and tighter business relationships** for a variety of purposes: process development, marketing, training and purchasing. Firms meet to discuss common problems and needs then, wherever appropriate, propose joint solutions. The **catalyst for collaboration** has varied across states. In some instances, it was simply learning about the Italian experience and taking action spontaneously; in other instances, it was a small incentive in the form of a challenge grant through the state or the Southern Technology Council; in still other instances, it was foundation support. Leadership came from a broker in a few instances, from a visionary SME owner in others. The response is generally favorable, in large part because SMEs find that the idea is not as foreign to small and rural businesses as one might expect. Most firms do work with others in various but random ways, and most welcome the opportunity to learn from each other and not feel so alone.

Interfirm cooperation has become one of the most widely discussed new concepts in rural industrial development

States have tried **three strategies** to encourage and stimulate interfirm cooperation. The first is **incentives for collaboration**, usually as challenge grants for group activities. In 1989, the Michigan Modernization Service requested proposals for collaboration involving three or more firms; grants were as large as $25,000. One example of the projects proposed was from a group of transformer and coil manufacturers that joined together in a purchasing network; another example was an association of foundries that collectively addressed a common solid waste disposal problem.

The second strategy is **restructuring existing service programs** so that staff become catalysts for network activities. In Pennsylvania, group services and flexible manufacturing networks were made part of the mission of the Industrial Resource Centers. The same charge was given the directors of Regional Technology Councils in Indiana and Maryland. In Oklahoma, it is anticipated that staff of the state's vocational-technical colleges, which already are working with SMEs, will take on much of the responsibility for facilitating networks.

The third strategy is **supporting individuals or organizations to act as network facilitators and help organize collaborative efforts.** No statewide attempt has

Oregon and Industrial Networks: Spotted Owls, Wooden Dowels

Forest products accounted for 36 percent of Oregon's manufacturing jobs and 7 percent of all wage and salary jobs in 1988. Up until the last few years, that single sector was healthy enough to make Oregon a relatively prosperous state. But two events—a slowdown in the U.S. economy that hit the home building industry particularly hard and new federal land use management to protect the habitat of the northern spotted owl—took millions of acres of woodland out of production. Predicting a loss of 11,000 jobs in the industry over the next five years, the state began to look for alternatives. One was to find ways to keep more value added in state.

In 1989, the Northwest Policy Center (NPC), a regional public policy think tank located at the University of Washington in Seattle, with a grant from the German Marshall Fund, took a group of legislators and state officials from Oregon and Washington to Europe. The purpose of the study tour was to investigate the flexible manufacturing networks through which small, artisan furniture companies in northern Italy were capturing large shares of world markets. Intrigued by the prospect of applying these European flexible manufacturing network experiences to add more value to the state's troubled wood products industry, the Oregon legislature commissioned NPC to prepare a report and make recommendations. In preparing its report, NPC looked at policies and practices in the wood products sector in other regions of the United States as well as in Europe. The NPC also talked directly with business owners, through a series of focus groups in Oregon and Washington. The report recommended various means to stimulate the industry, particularly emphasizing small and medium-sized enterprises working together.

The Oregon legislature shaped and molded the recommendations into comprehensive, ground-breaking legislation. The law was innovative because it: (1) took a "Third Wave" approach, using the private sector to operate the programs; (2) emphasized flexible manufacturing networks; and (3) provided enough funds to have a significant impact. The legislation establishes a Woods Products Competitiveness Corporation with a board composed of seven business people from the industry. The Corporation has been given state funds to allocate according to the act's provisions, which include training network brokers, providing challenge grants as incentives to form collaborative activities, giving service vouchers to firms for partial costs of services and with incentives for group services, and providing technical assistance through an industrial extension service. Before commencing the program, five of the directors visited European firms and found out first-hand how approaches based on collective action among small firms worked.

This new approach, with the private sector directing the use of funds and encouraging interfirm collaboration, will be tested. The careful planning, systematic approach, involvement of the private sector throughout the planning, support of key and knowledgeable legislators, and the availability of more than $2 million as incentives suggest that it will prove successful. The state, through other legislation, has adopted an exhaustive set of benchmarks to measure the program's performance, so it is likely that the legislature will know just how its investment is paying off at the end of a few years.

CONTACT:

Joe Cortright, Executive Officer
Joint Committee on Trade & Economic Development
Oregon Legislature
State Capitol, Room 13
Salem, Oregon 97310-1347
(503) 378-8811

been made to do this yet, although there are a number of local examples supported by private foundations. In rural areas of Washington, Montana and Minnesota, organizations have been chosen and awarded three-year grants to develop networks among local firms. In Washington's Olympic peninsula, WoodNet operates through an Economic Development Council to introduce secondary wood products firms to each other and urge them to think and act cooperatively. A short distance south, a fast-growing wood products cooperative is marketing products for dozens of artisan wood products firms, including through two cooperative-owned retail outlets.

Taking a Sector-specific Focus

Most state economic development programs, with the exception of ones for agriculture, ignore differences among sectors and address functional needs. Typically, one agency provides training, another capital, another export assistance, another technology information, and another management advice. States are beginning to realize they can provide the needed expertise best by concentrating on specific sectors. Just as the U.S. Departments of Commerce and Agriculture have offices or desks that follow a specific industrial sector or type of product, some states are looking at concentrating their expertise and efforts. They can either organize economic development around industries, as Illinois did, or identify institutions to support an industry. Some colleges have begun to focus on locally important industries, as well. Itawamba Community College in Tupelo, Mississippi, is a source of innovation for the local furniture industry, and Catawba Valley Community College in North Carolina provides technology and training to nearby manufacturers, which produce 30 percent of the nation's hosiery. An experimental project in New Jersey, designed by C. Richard Hatch, a consultant who has played a lead role in drawing attention to SMEs and opportunities for collaboration, establishes four technical colleges as sectoral hubs, organizing and coordinating a wide range of information and support agencies for one sector.

States are beginning to realize they can provide the needed expertise best by concentrating on specific sectors

Maine's Center for Technology Transfer: A Focused Approach

Maine, a rural state with only about 2,000 manufacturers, would not seem to be a key player in U.S. industrial competitiveness. Yet in the fall of 1991, Bob Dalton, director of the state's Center for Technology Transfer (CTT), traveled to Japan with a group led by Undersecretary of Commerce Bob White to observe the operations of Japan's manufacturing sector. Maine, in fact, has small but important metals and electronics sectors made up primarily of about 500 small firms, and the state recognizes the need to help them to innovate and modernize.

In 1988, the Maine Science and Technology Commission established the Center for Technology Transfer to address the needs of small and medium-sized metals and electronics manufacturers throughout the state. This was one of three state technology transfer centers, the other two targeted for biotechnology and aquaculture. The state grant, which was $300,000 in FY 1991, has to be matched from other sources, including fees for services and matches for challenge grants. CTT's host organization is the University of Maine system, but its advisory board is drawn from both the public and private sectors. Give that the budget supports only two full-time staff, the advisory board and committees are active participants. In 1991, members logged 1,100 hours of Center-related activity.

CTT's six services are: (1) demonstrating advanced technologies, (2) stimulating productivity improvement, (3) disseminating technical information, (4) monitoring emerging issues, (5) brokering industry needs and services and (6) facilitating interfirm networks and strategic alliances. Its market is the entire state, although practically all manufacturing there is south of Bangor. Lacking field staff, CTT reaches out through its publications and faculty at university branches.

At first, the program's designers expected that its contributions would come from more traditional technology transfer out the universities' research labs. It soon became clear, however, that SMEs' needs were much more basic, and CTT turned its attention to modernization, which Dalton believes is the key to the state's industrial growth but requires a change in the business culture. One mechanism the center uses to influence firm behavior is the challenge grant. These grants are used to encourage interfirm collaboration, or networks, particularly to develop products jointly. "Networks," Dalton says, "are inherent in all our activities. We've got to get companies to work more closely together." The grants are expected to be paid back to the Center if and when the product becomes profitable. In July 1991, CTT awarded four grants totalling $54,500. One grant, for example, supported the development of a new road sander by six businesses, another the design of a new sensor by three firms, and a third, the development of a special multi-purpose personal computer designed for people with disabilities.

CTT also is working to organize the state's electronics industry through an association that will eventually provide real services, perhaps modeled on the Maine Metal Products Association. It expected to publish a directory of member firms and hold its first association meeting in early 1992.

During 1992, New England's economic picture was bleak, and Maine's was no better. The state's budget deficit is putting a damper on all programs, including science and technology. CTT's budget for FY 1992 was reduced by 8.3 percent. This puts CTT, which never had a budget sufficient to meet the demand, in a survival mode. Paradoxically, the weak economy, according to Dalton, may inspire modernization and in the long run help stabilize industry. "Businesses are more eager for help and more willing to upgrade themselves for fear that there will not be a tomorrow."

Maine's Center for Technology Transfer represents an attempt by a very rural and sparsely populated state to focus on a couple of important industries, to utilize available resources, and to be a catalyst for change. Its funding is not sufficient for the task at hand, but its design and procedures are noteworthy.

CONTACT:
Robert Dalton, Executive Director
Center for Technology Transfer
59 Exeter Street
Portland, Maine 04102
(207) 780-4616

Expanding Extension Services

In 1980, only three colleges had a significant industrial extension service: North Carolina State University, Georgia Tech and Penn State University. During the mid- to late 1980s, industrial extension programs—sometimes called **technology extension** to provide a more contemporary and modern look—were established in about a dozen states. Most are staffed, however, by only a few engineers. One federal catalyst for new or expanded technology activities has been the Boehlert-Rockefeller grants provided in the Omnibus Trade and Competitiveness Act of 1988. The grants were designed to encourage states to establish new technology extension programs and have led to a proliferation of new programs. Nine awards were made in 1990, but the average size of the award is less than the equivalent of one professional person year.

One of the first grants went to the Tennessee Department of Economic and Community Development (TECD), which contracted with the University of Tennessee's Center for Industrial Services. The program's linchpin is the Tennessee Association of Small Business Services, which finds and initially counsels clients. Additional clientele are expected to be identified through seven TECD workshops across the state. A two-person team then is assigned to assess each client's opportunities to apply advanced technology. Another grant went to the Arkansas Science & Technology Authority (ASTA), which selected three Technology Assistance Service Providers (TASPs)—all located in college or university manufacturing centers in different regions of the state— one in Little Rock, one in Camden, and one in Fayetteville. In addition, ASTA named secondary TASPs at colleges in Jonesboro, Pine Bluff, and Russellville.

The federal government, amidst vigorous debate about the merits of a national industrial policy, is taking small steps—insufficient to address rural manufacturers on any significant scale but enough to entice states into taking action. The Omnibus Trade and Competitiveness Act of 1988, for instance, authorizes the National Institute of

The federal government is taking small steps to entice states into taking action

Standards and Technology to fund regional manufacturing technology centers (MTCs). The MTCs are aimed at helping SMEs overcome their reluctance to take advantage of advanced technologies developed at NIST in Gaithersburg, Maryland. In practice, however, MTCs seek to promote technology from a range of federal and commercial sources. Although the MTCs have not been funded at anywhere near the level anticipated in the authorizing legislation, they are stimulating states' interest in modernization and leveraging other resources, and

Mid-America Manufacturing Technology Center: Something Old, Something New

In April 1991, the Mid-America Manufacturing Technology Center (MAMTC) was established under a cooperative agreement between the National Institute of Standards and Technology and the Kansas Technology Enterprise Corporation. This marked the second round of manufacturing technology centers (MTCs) to be funded under the Omnibus Trade and Competitiveness Act of 1988 but, given that MAMTC serves a more sparsely populated area than the other four MTCs, it has taken a different approach to modernization services, integrating a wide array of existing programs and focusing their attention on SMEs.

Headquarters for MAMTC are in suburban Overland Park, Kansas, but six regional offices in Kansas and Missouri provide technical assistance to manufacturers in their territories: three of the offices are located in rural areas. Community colleges in Kansas and Missouri, the cooperative extension service, and the small business centers each have major roles to play. For example, MAMTC includes county cooperative extension agents in its field engineer training programs so they can learn to help rural SMEs identify problems or needs, and community colleges provide technical training to supplement the acquisition of new technologies or techniques.

To begin, MAMTC serves Kansas and four counties in Missouri, home to more than 4,000 manufacturing establishments. Resources it has acquired or expects to have soon include: two CIM demonstration centers; a telecommunications system to provide information to and links with SMEs; a mobile demonstration and training facility; and a management system to coordinate activities and broker technical and business services. MAMTC has 16 field engineers who provide one-on-one consultations, demonstrations, training, and industry networks to accomplish the program's objectives. The four areas on which it focused initially were CAD/CAM, quality, process planning, and electronic data interchange.

MAMTC will have a chance to learn from the experiences of the other three MTCs through the Modernization Forum, an organization governed and supported by the MTCs and NIST. In 1990, NIST selected the first three sites: the Great Lakes Manufacturing Technology Center (GLMTC) at Cuyahoga Community College's Unified Technologies Center in Cleveland; the Northeast Manufacturing Technology Center (NMTC) at Rensselear Polytechnic Institute in Albany, New York; and the Southeast Manufacturing Technology Center (SMTC) at the University of South Carolina. Each has taken a slightly different approach and, although each focuses primarily on its immediate surroundings, each has found ways to branch out geographically to reach more clients. SMTC, for example, operates in cooperation with the state system of technical colleges, which have sophisticated technology centers. GLMTC originally limited itself to the Cleveland area but is deploying teams of field engineers to work with the industrial resource centers in western Pennsylvania.

Funding for these centers in total is far less than authorized in the legislation. Further, by the end of the sixth year, each MTC is expected to be independent of federal support and operate on state and local funds and/or client fees. In theory, this is a sound program, although the scale is quite modest and expectations high. A 1991 report from the U.S. General Accounting Office stated that "the MTC program deserved continued support based on its promising start," but noted that "any measurement of the MTC program's impact should take into account its relatively small size and the nation's large manufacturing competitiveness problem."

CONTACT:

Paul Clay, Director
Mid-America Manufacturing Technology Center
10561 Barkley, Suite 602
Overland Park, Kansas 66212
(913) 649-4333

Arkansas Science and Technology Authority: Coordinating Resources

Arkansas, a rural state that ranks near the bottom on most economic indicators, has been willing to take risks on new and innovative programs to leap into the 21st Century. In 1983, the legislature established the Arkansas Science and Technology Authority (ASTA) to develop the state's technology resources. Under the leadership of president John Ahlen, ASTA began an array of programs to expand and commercialize the state's research, and by 1991 Arkansas ranked in the top ten (Corporation for Enterprise Development's Report Card on the States) in its science and technology programs.

In the last few years, ASTA and the state have increasingly turned their attention to helping Arkansas' manufacturing base modernize. First, a promotional grant program (a discretionary fraction of the higher education budget) was targeted to economic development centers at each of the universities, many of which tried to assist small manufacturers. Next, ASTA, in collaboration with the Southern Technology Council and with support from the Winthrop Rockefeller Foundation, began a demonstration project for flexible manufacturing networks. The first firms to organize established the Metalworking Connection, Inc., which has become a national model. Finally, the state won two awards from NIST for technology extension activities. The first, awarded in 1990, identified three Technology Assistance Service Providers (TASPs), all located in existing college or university manufacturing centers in different regions of the state, to work with ASTA to increase the use of technologies developed at federal laboratories. One was at the University of Arkansas in Little Rock; one at the Center for Competitive Manufacturing in Camden (SAU Tech, member of the Consortium for Manufacturing Competitiveness, which operates four mobile technology vans); and one at the University of Arkansas' Center for Technology Transfer in Fayetteville. In addition, ASTA named secondary TASPs at colleges in Jonesboro, Pine Bluff and Russellville. As part of that grant, the TASPs assisted 33 businesses—all but six of which were small firms.

The second grant, awarded to only two first-year winners in 1991, was to develop plans for a coordinated and comprehensive system of service providers—building a technology extension system from existing resources. The heads of ASTA, the Arkansas Industrial Development Commission, the Small Business Development Center, and the Department of Higher Education are forming a sub-cabinet to facilitate good working relationships. Project staff will host focus groups for providers across the state, establish memorandums of agreement with providers to participate in a statewide extension network, and develop, with advice from representative SMEs, an easily accessible database of extension services and resources and to encourage greater collaboration among firms and the formation of manufacturing networks.

CONTACT:
John Ahlen, President
Arkansas Science and Technology Authority
100 Main Street, Suite 450
Little Rock, Arkansas 72201
(501) 324-9006

NIST's technology extension awards have stimulated new programs in more than a dozen states. In 1991, the Senate passed the Critical Technologies Act of 1991, which support SMEs and includes provisions encouraging flexible manufacturing networks and authorizes (but has yet to appropriate) $50 million for technology extension.

Linking Community Colleges, Research-oriented Centers, and SMEs

Technical, community and four-year regional colleges are the most common sources of non-agricultural technology and technical assistance in rural areas. In some states, two-year colleges were founded to support economic development but are oriented toward recruitment and customized training. Regional colleges also are assuming greater responsibility for economic development, an increasing number are hosts to economic development centers. Part of Arkansas' higher education budget, for example, funds economic development centers, many of which operate as technology deployment outposts. Both two-year and regional colleges are beginning to realize a much greater potential in technology extension and demonstration for SMEs. The emerging concept of the advanced technology center is designed to bridge the gap between the SME and the more sophisticated and usually distant research centers.

Federal agencies, too, are beginning to recognize the potential of regional colleges. For example, program designers expected that Manufacturing Technology Centers would be housed with university or research center programs. But as a result of increasing links among training, modernization and technical colleges' close ties to SMEs, all MTCs work hand-in-hand with technical colleges. The Southeastern Manufacturing Technology Center, for instance, is a partnership between the state's technical colleges and the University of South Carolina. The Mid-America Manufacturing Technology Center uses community colleges as its satellite centers, and the Great Lakes Manufacturing Technology Center's headquarters are at Cuyahoga Community College in Cleveland.

All MTCs work hand-in-hand with technical colleges

The Consortium for Manufacturing Competitiveness: Technical Colleges on the Cutting Edge

Among the educational institutions with the capacity to support modernization, perhaps the most promising and most underutilized are the two-year colleges. Created in many states to support economic development, community and technical colleges are quietly rising to preeminence in technical education. With universities oriented toward cutting-edge research and high schools toward basic skills, the two-year college stands alone with a primary mission of encouraging economic development. As local institutions, they are more likely to be trusted by and accessible to small, rural manufacturers.

Some of the colleges, with strong industrial technology programs and sophisticated technology centers, have begun to realize a potential impact that extends farther than education and training, using their experience and expertise with new technologies to influence and support modernization efforts through extension and demonstration. Attesting to their technical expertise, IBM's CIM-Higher Education Consortium is directing more of its equipment to two-year colleges than to four-year colleges. In an attempt to capitalize on this potential and to develop it further, the Southern Technology Council organized a demonstration project, the Consortium for Manufacturing Competitiveness (CMC), comprised of colleges with outstanding industrial technology resources and programs from each of 14 southern states. The original design called for the colleges to work cooperatively to develop innovative approaches and to share their ideas and experiences with other colleges in their state. They were also charged with achieving greater economies of scale by offering services collectively rather than one-on-one. Due to the success of CMC and its companion program, the National Alliance for Manufacturing Productivity, (which was started at about the same time as CMC by Autodesk, Inc., a CAD software producer) NIST's manufacturing technology centers have come to rely heavily on the technical colleges to reach and assist SMEs.

After three years, CMC has become widely known for its innovative services and programs for SMEs. Each member college has found some special niche for working with small firms. For example:

- Kentucky's Somerset Community College developed a unique arrangement with the College of Engineering at the University of Kentucky and is jointly operating a mobile technology van (see Kentucky case study). The van travels to various remote sites to demonstrate process technologies and train workers.

- Southern Arkansas University Tech (SAU Tech) operates three such mobile vans, one for robotics, one for hydraulics and pneumatics, and one for CAD, CNC and PLC. The college hosts a "High Tech Week" which attracted 1,500 visitors in one year to rural southern Arkansas to see demonstrations at the college's flexible manufacturing cell.

- Hagerstown Junior College in western Maryland has assembled one of the most advanced manufacturing centers in the region for machining companies (producing both parts and equipment). It offers computer-integrated production capacity on a shared time basis. In addition to regular training activities, 12 firms serve on the advisory committee and another 12 share the equipment. The college is also working with the state's Western Regional Technology Council and seven manufacturers to develop a Technical Innovation Center.

- Chattanooga State Technical College, which has one of the nation's most advanced facilities, has a Cooperative Demonstration Program in computer integrated manufacturing. Named a regional support center for CIM by IBM, the college regularly hosts breakfast meetings that draw rural small manufacturers to learn about new concepts.

- In Tupelo, Mississippi, the northeast corner of the state, Itawamba Community College has designed and built a state-of-the-art Automated Furniture Manufacturing Technology Center to serve the needs of one of the region's most important industries. The Center focuses particularly on furniture upholstery, which has been one of the most labor-intensive operations in the industry. It is used not only for training and retraining, but to demonstrate the potential of computer-aided design, grading, marking, spreading, and cutting of fabrics.

A number of colleges have expanded their effectiveness by introducing the concept of flexible manufacturing networks:

- Florida's Okaloosa-Walton Community College has strong training programs but little technical equipment, so it has concentrated on facilitating flexible manufacturing networks. Following a one-day CMC workshop, which featured presentations at the college by leading experts from the United States and Emilia-Romagna in Italy, local SMEs organized to form the Technology Coast Engineering and Manufacturing Network. Through regular meetings, the firms have shared the costs of specialized information, jointly bid on contracts, and generally re-established collaborative activities. Support has come from Florida and the Gulf Power Corporation.

- The Bevill Center, a joint project of Gadsden State Community College and the University of Alabama, also has introduced flexible manufacturing networks. A sophisticated training facility for local tooling and machining companies, the center began a new organization to share resources, develop new technologies and exchange information. Another group of firms is planning a collaborative apprenticeship training program.

- Wytheville Community College in western Virginia is organizing the wood products industry. Working through the state's Center for Innovative Technology, the college has become a focal point for technical information for the industry and, in mid-1992, was organizing SMEs into networks for collaborative production, which will include the joint investment by 10 small firms in a state-of-the-art kiln drying company. This company will add value to the cooperating firms and allow them to control the quality of raw material needed in the area.

The Consortium for Manufacturing Competitiveness effectively demonstrates the ability of technical colleges to assume new and expanded responsibilities for industrial modernization. But the true test of an effective demonstration is the extent to which it affects practice elsewhere. To be replicated on a larger scale, states will have to acknowledge and provide support for this function. To date, most states will only fund colleges on the basis of full-time equivalent enrollments, and the institutions that want to provide technology extension and demonstration for their manufacturing base are forced to find additional revenues through various entrepreneurial schemes. A few states are adopting the CMC model. The Florida legislature appropriated funds to four additional colleges to become manufacturing technology centers, and Oklahoma is redefining the role of selected faculty in its vocational-technical colleges as technology and innovation brokers.

CONTACT:
Stuart Rosenfeld, President
Consortium for Manufacturing Competitiveness
c/o Regional Technology Strategies, Inc.
P.O. Box 9005
Chapel Hill, North Carolina 27515-9005
(919) 933-6699

Youth Apprenticeship

One of the most intriguing ideas for supporting modernization is youth apprenticeship, an old European program retrofit to the new U.S. economy. Once a large and important part of America's education and training enterprise, apprenticeship has shrunk to about 3 percent of the workforce—mostly adults in construction trades. European nations, most notably Germany and the Scandinavian countries, use apprenticeship to train job entrants for most jobs in industry and commerce. It is the most common educational experience of German youth and highly regarded by managers, about 80 percent of whom have gone through the program themselves. The idea of an apprenticeship that begins at age 16 and possibly extends through postsecondary education is capturing the attention and imagination of U.S. policy-makers. In 1991, Arkansas, Oregon and Wisconsin enacted legislation authorizing youth apprenticeships, and Pennsylvania began a pilot program.

European nations use apprenticeship to train job entrants for most jobs in industry and commerce

But even as states are taking their first steps toward establishing youth apprenticeship programs, some colleges and trade associations are taking matters into their own hands and designing local programs. In southern Arkansas, two regional colleges are working with the Metalworking Connection, a group of more than 50 SMEs, to plan an apprenticeship program. In Gadsden, Alabama, the Bevill Center for Advanced Manufacturing Technology is setting up a shared apprenticeship program with a group of small machine tool companies. And in Maryland, MechTech, Inc., has been formed as a non-profit corporation of companies (10 members in 1992) to create a program with Catonsville Community College to train apprentice machinists. The **common thread** in each of these is that **apprentices will rotate** among firms to broaden their education and experience base.

Interesting Ideas from Europe

Many of the newest ideas making their way into U.S. public policy originated in Europe. Conversely, many innovative programs in the United State are being adapted to European conditions. This **cross-fertilization** has accelerated in recent years, with more and more American policy-makers and practitioners traveling overseas, not to seek new businesses to locate in their state but to identify new ideas that can improve public policy. Incentive grants from the German Marshall Fund of the United States have played an important part in this cross fertilization by encouraging travel and information exchange. It is no longer unusual to find representatives of other nations at U.S. conferences on industrial modernization and vice versa. Nations that have had a prominent, if not profound, impact on U.S. policy are Italy, Denmark, Sweden and Germany. In Europe, 1.9 million firms are listed as small- and medium-sized manufacturing enterprises.[4] The Commission of the European Communities now gives SMEs high priority, and virtually every relevant program for industry must include provisions to address the SME needs. Among the European Community programs are CRAFT (Cooperative Research Action for Technology), which provides funds for precompetitive research that involves five or more SMEs and a research institution; BRITE (Basic Research in Industrial Technology for Europe) has a set-aside for SMEs; and COMETT (a program for university-industry cooperation) urges universities to work with SMEs as partners. Even EUREKA! seeks out SMEs for multi-national research initiatives.

In Europe, 1.9 million firms are listed as small- and medium-sized manufacturing enterprises

Two success stories, already mentioned, have ignited interest in Europe. One is the modern, tightly interwoven, artisan industrial economy of Emilia-Romagna, and the other is Germany's technical training and technology transfer programs. Italy is the first stop for many U.S. delegations that are eager to learn about its success in traditional industries which, in this country, are in a decline that many experts considered inevitable and unstoppable. Denmark is of interest, first because of its well-articulated technology infrastructure and second because it invested heavily in adapting northern Italy's production system to a less densely populated industrial landscape and a different culture. Other Scandinavian nations have attracted U.S. policy-makers because of their history of cooperative production, production cooperatives and exemplary labor-management-government relationships.

Danish networks: Denmark, with slightly more than five million citizens and about the same percent employment in manufacturing as most U.S. states is hardly typical with respect to its modernization policies. With thousands of small manufacturers and only a handful of large producers, the Danish manufacturing sector **must rely heavily on its wits** to compete. Danish leaders studied Italy's success and were impressed with the way cooperation and a **strong support infrastructure** had brought success to Emilia-Romagna. The Danish government decided this region's experience was Denmark's best chance to strengthen its SME base. The government committed itself to encouraging Danish industry to adopt the kind of behaviors that gave Italy its edge. The Ministry of Trade and Industry authorized $25 million to induce SMEs to work with one another, and, working with consultant C. Richard Hatch, devised a scheme that included educating the public, selecting and training "network brokers," and offering three stages of incentives for collaboration. At the same time, the government contracted for an evaluation of how broadly the concept was accepted, the impacts on firms' competitiveness, *This program succeeded on all measures* and sustainability. This program succeeded on all measures: More than 3,000 firms had engaged in networking activities after 18 months; of those interviewed, most could show either lower costs, expanded markets or increased productivity.

The Danish networking program was not, however, an isolated modernization program. To support the effort, the ministry called on the Danish Technological Institute, a private business founded to support technology development in 1906; Technology Information Centers in every county, each of those counties with "extension agents" providing information; decentralized applied research centers; and technology application centers located in seven technical colleges. Thus, Denmark has a very comprehensive, accessible, well-organized infrastructure to support its new modernization initiatives.

Emilia-Romagna's hubs: As described above, Emilia-Romagna is a region in the heart of "Third Italy." In 1974, one of the first acts of the region's new government was to create ERVET, a development agency. ERVET soon found its niche with sector-specific hubs for the region's most important industries. Firms that use and must pay for the hubs' services define hub functions. Today, ERVET administers 12 centers—10 for specific industries and 2 addressing the cross-cutting needs of computer-integrated manufacturing (ASTER) and export promotion (SVEX). One of the centers, CITER, is located in the small city of Carpi, the heart of the region's very modern and competitive knitwear industry; more than 2,000 artisan firms are located in the vicinity, and only 17 have more than 50 employees. Citer provides the latest market trend and fashion information to the firms, very few of which could afford this information if they had to purchase it individually. CITER has also developed a CAD system, called CITERA, for the garment industry, and it hosts workshops on technical and management issues. CERMET is a center that helps the large metals industry prepare to meet new European standards by developing and offering new metals and process testing methods. A third center, CERMICA, provides similar services plus research and technical assistance to the ceramic tile industry. Membership fees from firms, trade associations, chambers of commerce, and unions provide the bulk of support for ERVET's centers, although they are not yet completely self-sufficient.

Germany's chambers of commerce: Chambers of commerce are important **catalysts for modernization** in Germany. While chamber membership is mandatory in Germany, the services the association offers are substantial. In Aachen, for instance, the chamber brokers technology transfer activities between the universities and businesses, sponsors seminars for SMEs about R&D opportunities, organizes institute visits, and makes business referrals. Chamber staffs also consult directly with businesses to solve minor technical problems or to assist in negotiations between small firms and larger firms; firms trust the Chamber to preserve confidentiality.

While chamber membership is mandatory in Germany, the services the association offers are substantial

To encourage SMEs to use these consulting services, the Ministry of Economic Affairs pays 75 percent of the cost of the first five days and 50 percent of the next 15 days. The chamber also publishes a monthly magazine to promote opportunities like industrial partnering (and allow companies to advertise for network partners) or new products that are available for licensing. Most German chambers also act as the funding agent for the government and operate apprenticeship training programs, arranging placements and monitoring progress.

Chapter 4. Emerging Issues

As Chapter 3 illustrates, examples and methods of effective practice for rural manufacturing modernization have been developed in several states and nations. These programs' experience provides important lessons and insights for policy and practice. However, the field of manufacturing modernization is still a relatively new one. Few rural areas, if any, could claim that a fully comprehensive system has been developed. Policy and practice need to evolve to overcome a series of important issues and challenges facing rural manufacturing modernization. This chapter examines these issues.

Policy and practice need to evolve

Scale and intensity is one of the most critical issues facing current rural manufacturing modernization efforts. In general, most industrial extension and modernization programs do not have enough resources to reach large numbers of SMEs in their areas, and usually their assistance is limited to a few days each year for those firms they do reach. Adding federal and state resources together, the United States spends only about $70 million a year on industrial extension. On top of that, federal and state policies continue to emphasize research and technology development, rather then technology deployment. Compared with Japan, the U.S. spends much less on industrial extension activities, has far fewer field staff and program centers, and has a poorer geographic coverage of service provision. The majority of rural areas in the United States still lack any kind of organized industrial extension and modernization programs.

A second and related issue is **stability and long-term policy support**. With only one or two exceptions, industrial extension and modernization programs lack institutional and financial stability and have weak long-term policy support. The well-regarded Michigan Modernization Service was terminated by a new governor, and several other effective programs have faced budget reductions. In other cases, the institutional base of programs has changed, switching from one agency to another. This instability, in part, reflects the newness of industrial extension and modernization; time is still needed for things to "settle down." But perhaps more fundamentally, there continues to be uncertainty in government, in education and training systems, and in industry itself about the importance of rural industrial modernization, about what it is and who should do it, and about the relationship between modernization and economic development.

There continues to be uncertainty in government, in education and training systems, and in industry itself about the importance of rural industrial modernization

Third, **issues of program context** persist in rural industrial extension and modernization. Rural areas are quite diverse, ranging from the traditional rural manufacturing valleys of New England to the more industrialized rural South. Some rural areas are close to metropolitan areas and can use urban technology services, while other rural areas are remote and do not have the advantages of easy access. Relatively high levels of workforce education can be found in some areas, such as in rural Minnesota, in contrast to the lesser educated workforce found in parts of Louisiana or Mississippi. Rural modernization programs need to account for these differences in their design and develop approaches which will work under specific local conditions. But this is often easier said than done. Industrial extension and modernization programs work best where basic public and private services—such as education, transportation, communications, utilities and banking —are already working well. The programs can then play a critical role in enhancing the value of the services to manufacturers and in building or strengthening organizational infrastructures, such as local trade associations. But in rural areas with very severe community development problems and inadequate basic public and private services, much more than industrial extension and manufacturing modernization will be needed to make a difference.

Industrial extension and modernization programs work best where basic public and private services are already working well

An associated and fourth problem is **program linkage**. The problems of small and mid-sized manufacturers are often complex and involve all aspects of the business, so industrial extension and modernization programs need to be well linked with complementary training, management, financial and other business assistance programs. For example, before introducing new technology, a company may need to upgrade its job bidding and estimating procedures. When new technology is introduced, workforce training is invariably required, and management assistance may be necessary. From the company's perspective, these services should be provided seamlessly, without bureaucracy getting in the way, and in various mixes according to the specific situation—a level of coordination that is hard to realize. When companies are located in rural communities, complementary business and training service centers are often distant. Moreover, these distant centers and institutions have their own mandates, procedures and "turf," which can make coordination problematic. One answer to these problems is for industrial extension and modernization services to find ways to coordinate and develop private sources of business services.

Find ways to coordinate and develop private sources of business services

Questions about program design, tools and evaluations present further challenges to rural industrial extension and modernization strategies and make up the fifth issue. How can programs be tailored to varied rural industries, areas, and conditions? What tools and methods should be used? How can and should programs be evaluated? In general, the field of industrial modernization lacks research, analytical tools, and assessment techniques. It is costly for individual programs to provide this themselves, and efforts are often duplicated as individual programs develop their own company assessment techniques. There are also unresolved issues about the criteria for judging industrial modernization success. Political pressure, at times, forces programs to try to count jobs saved or created, but this is a very inadequate measure of modernization. Counting the number of companies served is another frequently used measure, but this may say little about a program's quality or effect. Moreover, such measures may be a disadvantage for rural programs, since it is easier to serve (and count) more geographically concentrated urban manufacturers.

The field of industrial modernization lacks research, analytical tools, and assessment techniques

Finally, but perhaps most important, there is the issue of **stimulating systemic change**. Industrial extension and modernization services which address specific problems in individual firms are important but ultimately limited. There are too many firms and far too many individual problems for this one-on-one approach to modernization to tackle. Ultimately, modernization strategies must set firms on longer-term upgrading paths, stimulating them to enhance their internal capabilities for problem solving and technological development and their collaborative linkages with other small and mid-sized enterprises, suppliers and vendors, private and public service providers, and customers. As an essential foundation for this, manufacturers need to make a paradigm shift, switching from an older, narrow view of production to a newer, more global view. The significant personal and institutional changes this shift implies will be particularly difficult to achieve in rural areas, where experience is more limited, managers may be more conservative, and change is resisted. This is a difficult challenge for modernization programs. Solving individual problems is simpler to do and arguably easier to justify to elected officials than fostering systemic changes in the rural manufacturing culture. Nonetheless, the ultimate judge of modernization initiatives' effectiveness will surely be the extent to which they can help seed these systemic changes.

The significant personal and institutional changes this shift implies will be particularly difficult to achieve in rural areas

Chapter 5. Steps to Modernization

As evidence of program effectiveness accumulates, principles for designing state programs and information pertaining to elements that lead to success are becoming clearer. Many reinforce previously cited characteristics of best practices. The steps are: (1) build constituency and leadership; (2) map local economies, including linkages among firms, and target sectors; (3) identify and coordinate resources and services; (4) involve SMEs; (5) build scale; and (6) establish procedures for accountability.[5] It is important, for example, to know a state's political environment and **build constituencies** among government, community organizations, trade associations, labor organizations, SMEs, and large producers. If there is no state leadership to build such constituencies, it must emerge from the process. No program succeeds without strong, even evangelistic, leadership. Building an inventory of the state's capabilities and making sure that **existing resource providers are involved and coordinated** are important parts of the process. And to have the maximum impact, a state ought to be able to map its economy, including the linkages among firms, then **target its investments to key critical sectors**. This requires not only economic analysis but surveying firms to identify their suppliers and customers.

No program succeeds without strong, even evangelistic, leadership

SMEs, who are not used to looking at the public sector as a helper much less a partner, have to be actively engaged in the process. Therefore, it is absolutely essential to **involve SMEs early and in all stages**, in focus groups and as members of advisory boards and allow the customers to guide the process. In some places and for some industries, trade associations may be able to represent SMEs, although such representation is rare in rural areas.

The public sector may achieve its greatest value as catalyst for change and be most effective by providing incentives for preferred and innovative behavior

The public sector may achieve its greatest value as catalyst for change and be most effective by providing incentives for preferred and innovative behavior. Its programs, however, must be at a scale that can make a difference. To achieve scale, **modernization must be**

debated and discussed as an economic development policy, not a technology policy. Finally, **accountability procedures** must be designed, benchmarks designated from the start and baseline information collected continually for later assessments of outcomes. New programs' values must be demonstrated to the satisfaction of legislators, as well as program beneficiaries.

Although many excellent new practices are noted in this book, none really has the scale to meet the needs of the entire nation's manufacturing base. The best programs can reach only a small number of a state's manufacturers with little more than access to information. Most states and localities continue to view modernization as a technical program that may reduce the number of jobs, not as an economic or rural development program that leads to job creation. Because of this misguided vision, states and communities have been unwilling to allocate to modernization even a small portion of what they offer branch plants as subsidies to locate or budget advertising to promote tourism. The federal government expresses interest in helping SMEs, but has not committed anywhere near the funds needed to deliver or even leverage services. And where the federal government does invest, it expects programs to become self-sufficient far too soon.

States must look at federal funding as short-term grants rather than as the foundation of new, ongoing programs

As a result, states must look at federal funding as short-term grants rather than as the foundation of new, ongoing programs. The U.S. Department of Agriculture is becoming interested in modernization and has a memorandum of understanding with NIST for a joint effort, but the effort has not been clearly defined yet and too few dollars have been assigned.

Some observers believe that states and the federal government's reluctance to support modernization heavily may be a blessing in disguise, forcing states to turn to the principal of **"Third Wave" economic development.** In this paradigm, the private sector delivers services and the market drives demand, but there is a clear role for the public sector as catalyst and broker, and it is held accountable for its efforts. In the best and most promising practices, government agencies listen to their clients; are catalysts for change and innovation and are responsible for a support infrastructure; work to change SMEs' attitudes toward each other and the public sector to enhance cooperation, learning, and partnerships; and insure accessibility of services to firms in small and rural communities. This, in fact, constitutes an **ad hoc industrial policy** in which states are leading the federal government and for which bipartisan support is mounting. The best and most promising programs and the experiences of individual states establish a frame of reference for formulating new and more effective national and regional industrial competitiveness strategies.

This constitutes an ad hoc industrial policy in which states are leading the federal government

Endnotes

1. One result was the federal government's STS program, which led to the formation, for instance, of Pennsylvania's PENNTAP and Georgia Tech's and North Carolina State University's industrial extension service. Funding ended in 1969, although the authorization is still in effect.

2. Different sectors have different needs for various technologies. Most SMEs surveyed by the CMC, however, were in metals or plastics sectors and have generally similar production equipment needs.

3. The state-wide Michigan Modernization Service undoubtably would have been included as a best practice if it had not been ended by the state administration.

4. Europe's classification scheme includes many direct services to manufacturing, such as software and engineering, and consulting firms and construction.

5. Much of this section borrows from principles developed independently by consultants Brian Bosworth and Niels Christian Nielsen of the Danish Technological Institute.

Selected Resources

Best, Michael. 1990. *The New Competition: Institutions of Industrial Restructuring* Cambridge, MA: Harvard University Press.

Clarke, Marianne K. and Eric Dobson. 1989. *Promoting Technology Excellence: The Role of State and Federal Extension Activities.* Washington, DC: National Governors' Association.

Dertouzos, Michael L., Richard K. Lester, and Robert M. Solow. 1989. *Made in America: Regaining the Competitive Edge.* Cambridge, MA: MIT Press.

National Coalition for Advanced Manufacturing. 1990. *Industrial Modernization: An American Imperative.* New York, NY: Thoman Publishing Company.

Northdurft, William. 1992. *Lessons from the Expert Masters: How Europe Helps Small Firms Become Exporters.* To be published by the Brookings Institution.

Office of Technology Assessment. 1990. *Making Things Better: Competing in Manufacturing.* Washington, DC: U.S. Government Printing Office.

_____. 1990. *Worker Training: Competing in the New Economy.* Washington, DC: U.S. Government Printing Office.

Osborne, David. 1988. *Laboratories of Democracy.* Cambridge, MA: Harvard Business School Press.

Palmintera, Diana. 1989. *Best Practices in European Innovation Development.* Washington, DC: EDA Project No. 99-07-13710, Economic Development Administration, U.S. Department of Commerce.

Piore, Michael J. and Charles F. Sabel. 1984. *The Second Industrial Divide: Possibilities for Prosperity.* New York, NY: Basic Books.

Porter, Michael. 1990. *The Competitive Advantage of Nations*. New York, NY: Free Press.

Pyke, Frank, G. Becattini, and W. Sengenbrenner. 1990. *Industrial Districts and Inter-firm Co-operation in Italy*. Geneva, Switzerland: International Institute for Labour Studies.

Rosenfeld, Stuart. 1992. *Competitive Manufacturing: New Strategies for Regional Development*. Piscataway, NJ: CUPR Press.

Shapira, Philip. 1990. *Modernizing Manufacturing: New Policies to Build Industrial Extension Services*. Washington, DC: Economic Policy Institute.

U.S. General Accounting Office. 1991. *Technology Transfer: Federal Efforts to Enhance the Competitiveness of Small Manufacturers*, GAO/RCED-92-30. Washington, DC: U.S. Government Printing Office.

Acknowledgments

This book draws on the experience and expertise of many people who are responsible for or who study state industrial policies in the United States. Many of the ideas and perspectives were drawn from the comments of participants in an intensive two-day workshop in August 1991, named in the next section. We would also like to thank The Aspen Institute's State Policy Program and the German Marshall Fund for their active support and encouragement. The judgments and final analysis, however, are the sole responsibilities of the authors.

We want to particularly thank Niels Christian Nielsen of the Danish Technological Institute for joining us from Europe and for his insightful contributions at the workshop; Julie Tenney, Carol Conway, and Linda Hoke of the Southern Growth Policies Board (SGPB) who, in addition to being workshop participants, read and commented on the draft; Kirsten Nyrop, secretary of economic development in Louisiana, who reviewed the final manuscript; Elaine Kelly and Leai Ho Smith of SGPB for their administrative assistance and with the meeting and bookkeeping; and Rosalyn Voige Demaree for her fine editing of the final manuscript.

Workshop Participants

John Ahlen
 President
 Arkansas Science and Technology Council
 Little Rock, Arkansas

David L. Barkley
 Professor
 Agriculture and Applied Economics
 Clemson University
 Clemson, South Carolina

Brian Bosworth
 Consultant
 Providence, Rhode Island

Harry Bowie
 President
 Delta Foundation
 Greenville, Mississippi

Rick Carlisle
 Senior Fellow
 Corporation for Enterprise Development–South
 Durham, North Carolina

Christopher M. Coburn
 Director
 Public Technology Programs
 Battelle Institute
 Columbus, Ohio

Mary Coleman
 Professor
 Jackson State University
 Branden, Mississippi

Sally Bay Cornwell
 Vice President
 Longmont Area Chamber of Commerce
 Longmont, Colorado

Ken Deavers
  Director
  Economic Research Service
  U.S. Department of Agriculture
  Washington, D.C.

David Dodson
  Vice President
  MDC, Inc.
  Chapel Hill, North Carolina

Irwin Feller
  Director
  Institute for Policy Research and Evaluation
  Penn State University
  University Park, Pennsylvania

DeWitt John
  Director
  State Policy Program
  The Aspen Institute
  Washington, D.C.

Donald R. Johnson
  Director
  Industrial Technology Services
  National Institute of Standards and Technology
  Gaithersburg, Maryland

James F. Johnson
  Director
  Virginia Cooperative Extension Service
  Virginia Tech
  Blacksburg, Virginia

Kris W. Kimel
  Executive Director
  Kentucky Science and Technology Council
  Lexington, Kentucky

Jacques Koppel
  President
  Greater Minnesota Corporation
  Minneapolis, Minnesota

Ted Maher
    National Program Leader
    Cooperative Extension Service
    U.S. Department of Agriculture
    Washington, D.C.

Niels Christian Nielsen
    Director–Corporate Strategy
    Danish Technological Institute
    Arhus, Denmark

Kirsten A. Nyrop
    Secretary of Economic Development
    State of Louisiana
    Baton Rouge, Louisiana

David Patterson
    President
    Tennessee Technology Foundation
    Knoxville, Tennessee

William E. Porter
    Vice President
    CENTECH
    Silver Spring, Maryland

Stuart Rosenfeld
    Director
    Southern Technology Council
    Research Triangle Park, North Carolina

Leslie Schneider
    Director
    Tufts University Manufacturing Resource Center
    College of Engineering
    Medford, Massachusetts

Philip Shapira
    Professor
    School of Public Policy
    Georgia Institute of Technology
    Atlanta, Georgia

Paul Sommers
  Research Director
  Northwest Policy Center,
  University of Washington
  Seattle, Washington

Linda Warren Swann
  Associate Director
  Alabama Resource Center
  Alabama Power Company
  Birmingham, Alabama

Audrey S. Theis
  Assistant Secretary
  Maryland Department of Economic and Employment
    Development
  Baltimore, Maryland

J. Trent Williams
  Vice President
  Louisiana Partnership for Technology and Innovation
  Baton Rouge, Louisiana

About the Authors

Stuart A. Rosenfeld is President of Regional Technology Strategies, Inc., a tax-exempt non-profit organization in Chapel Hill, North Carolina. He is also a senior policy fellow for the Southern Growth Policies Board, where he previously served as deputy director and originator and director of the Southern Technology Council. Dr. Rosenfeld has worked for General Electric Company and the National Institute of Education and directed a private alternative elementary school in Vermont. He holds a B.S. in chemical engineering cum laude from the University of Wisconsin and an Ed.D. in education policy from Harvard University. Dr. Rosenfeld is an adjunct professor at the University of North Carolina's School of City and Regional Planning and author of *Competitive Manufacturing: New Strategies for Regional Development.*

Philip Shapira is an Assistant Professor in the School of Public Policy at Georgia Institute of Technology, where he teaches and conducts research on economic and regional development, industrial restructuring and competitiveness, and technology policy in the United States, Japan, and Europe. Dr. Shapira was previously Research Assistant Professor at West Virginia University's Regional Research Institute and a Congressional Fellow and Analyst with the Office of Technology Assessment of the United States Congress. He holds a Ph.D. in City and Regional Planning from the University of California, Berkeley.

Trent Williams, an economist, is Vice President of the Louisiana Partnership for Technology and Innovation. The Louisiana Partnership is a private, not-for-profit corporation which specializes in pre-seed investments for technology-intensive business start-ups and university-based technological opportunities. The Louisiana Partnership also serves as technology policy advisor to Louisiana's governors and legislature. Prior to joining the Partnership, Mr. Williams was Vice President of Gulf South Research Institute and Undersecretary of the Louisiana Department of Commerce.

The Best Practices Series

How can states attempt to address problems of competitiveness, equity, and quality of life, especially in rural communities? The Best Practices series is a tool kit of ideas, research findings, and program models for state officials and others who work at the state level. The series is supported by the W.K. Kellogg Foundation and the Ford Foundation through the State Policy Program of The Aspen Institute. Each book is prepared by a team of experts, drawing on discussions among experts from community groups, business, government, universities, and non-profit organizations.

The first six books of the series will be:

Business Finance as a Tool for Development
by Deborah H. Markley with Katharine McKee

Designing Development Strategies in Small Towns
by Glen Pulver and David Dodson

Gearing Up for Success: Organizing a State for Rural Development
by David W. Sears, John M. Redman, Richard L. Gardner, and Stephen J. Adams

Smart Firms in Small Towns
by Stuart Rosenfeld with Philip Shapira and Trent Williams

Utilities and Rural Industries: New Partnerships for Development*
by Charles Bartsch and Diane De Vaul

States and Rural Development*
by Ron Ferguson and DeWitt John

*Forthcoming